PENGUIN BOOKS

The ^NEW Parent
CODE

Marilynn McLachlan has a degree in education and has worked with children and adolescents in Australia and New Zealand. Her roles have included regular classroom teaching, teaching children with special needs, and working with adolescents in self-esteem, drugs and alcohol, and sex education programmes in Sydney high schools. She is presently living in Auckland city with her four children and husband, Tony, who is head of performing arts at a local high school.

*For all the Mums and Dads who are doing their best
and making a difference in their children's lives
and therefore our nation.*

The *New* Parent CODE

12 Vital Clues to Achieving Modern Family Sanity

MARILYNN McLACHLAN

PENGUIN BOOKS

PENGUIN BOOKS

Published by the Penguin Group
Penguin Group (NZ), cnr Airborne and Rosedale Roads, Albany,
Auckland 1310, New Zealand (a division of Pearson New Zealand Ltd)
Penguin Group (USA) Inc., 375 Hudson Street,
New York, New York 10014, USA
Penguin Group (Canada), 10 Alcorn Avenue, Toronto,
Ontario, Canada M4V 3B2 (a division of Pearson Penguin Canada Inc.)
Penguin Books Ltd, 80 Strand, London, WC2R 0RL, England
Penguin Ireland, 25 St Stephen's Green,
Dublin 2, Ireland (a division of Penguin Books Ltd)
Penguin Group (Australia), 250 Camberwell Road, Camberwell,
Victoria 3124, Australia (a division of Pearson Australia Group Pty Ltd)
Penguin Books India Pvt Ltd, 11, Community Centre,
Panchsheel Park, New Delhi – 110 017, India
Penguin Books (South Africa) (Pty) Ltd, 24 Sturdee Avenue,
Rosebank, Johannesburg 2196, South Africa

Penguin Books Ltd, Registered Offices: 80 Strand, London, WC2R 0RL, England

First published by Penguin Group (NZ), 2005
1 3 5 7 9 10 8 6 4 2

Copyright © Marilynn McLachlan 2005

The right of Marilynn McLachlan to be identified as the author of this work in terms
of section 96 of the Copyright Act 1994 is hereby asserted.

Designed by Mary Egan
Typeset by Egan-Reid Ltd
Printed in Australia by McPherson's Printing Group

ISBN 0 14 301966 X
A catalogue record for this book is available
from the National Library of New Zealand.

www.penguin.co.nz

CONTENTS

INTRODUCTION

On a pleasant, sunny afternoon in April 2004, I set myself up on a blanket in the back garden and penned a letter to the Prime Minister, Helen Clark.

There was no forethought or planning involved. I just felt I had been pushed to my limits emotionally, physically and financially, and could not understand what was happening in New Zealand society that was making it so increasingly difficult to raise a family. I covered a number of issues in my letter – student loan debt, medical costs, lack of support for mothers and living expenses.

I could not understand why our family received little or no support when we were paying our taxes, paying off student loan debt, Tony was teaching the next generation, I was at home raising four members of the next generation, Tony was a volunteer ambulance officer – all things that I believed were contributing to the betterment of New Zealand society.

We lived frugally, yet our house was in need of repair (the kitchen and bathroom ceilings were caving in) and paint. With increasing debt, I had come to the conclusion that we couldn't afford our $80,000 mortgage (and repairs and rates and insurance) and would therefore need to sell.

We stressed about putting food on the table. We avoided going to the doctor because of the high cost. We purchased everything second-hand. But still we were going backwards.

I couldn't understand why it was the right of a woman without a partner to be able to stay at home with her children until they reached 14 years old, but the same right was not given to a woman with a working partner. I could not understand why my family constituted 'the wealthy' in terms of receiving health care, and yet each visit to the doctor was beyond our means.

From where I sat in my corner of the world, it seemed that investing millions of dollars of taxpayers' money in television stations or a black boat did not make sense when there were so many people struggling on a day-to-day basis.

I wrote to Helen Clark because I was so desperate that I went straight to the top. I wanted, indeed needed, some answers about what was going wrong.

When my husband Tony returned from work I read him the letter and told him that I was going to send it. No comment from him initially, but when pushed he said, 'Sign it McLachlan', meaning, 'I am not sure about this, please use your maiden name.'

We had a laugh and then I hopped on the Internet to search for relevant email addresses. I found the address for Helen Clark and many other MPs. I also sent a copy to the *Sunday Star-Times*. Within half an hour I received a short email from Helen Clark's office telling me that my email had been received, that she was busy and would reply to me within 21 days. It was one of those generic, auto replies that meant nobody had actually read my email, and that they'd get round to it one day.

You know, I never did get a reply from her.

The following day, a Friday, I received a phone call from Cate Brett, the editor of the *Sunday Star-Times*, telling me that they had received the letter and asking if I would be prepared to be interviewed by the *SST*. I replied that I would be happy to, and she said they would call again on Tuesday and arrange for someone to interview me at home in Waihi.

Come Wednesday afternoon, journalist Donna Chisholm and photographer David White arrived on our doorstep. Anyone who has ever met Donna would agree that she has eyes that seem to look right inside you, an intelligence that is admirable at the same time as it is petrifying, and an eye for detail that reminded me of a highly trained, highly capable police investigator. David and Donna spent the day with our family, stayed at a local motel and showed up for the 6 a.m. routine the following morning.

To be honest, I'm used to my privacy. In writing the letter to the Prime Minister I had left open for scrutiny some of the most intimate and private details of our lives. While I felt sick to my stomach most of the time, I answered the questions and was as honest as possible about what our life was like. I had no objective except to share our story, as New Zealanders who apparently 'had it all'. I knew what I was doing may be controversial, but I had absolutely no idea about the degree to which the controversy would swell.

As Sunday drew closer, I became more and more nervous about what would happen. Donna and I communicated almost hourly in order to clarify bits of information. On Saturday morning, our family travelled to Auckland because my parents were arriving for a visit from Australia. We visited the team at the *SST*. Cate and Donna were highly supportive – both warning me that I would receive numerous calls the next day, but also saying they believed I could handle it.

If you've ever stood next to Donna and Cate, you know you are dealing with two very strong women. If they thought I could handle it, I could. I kept these words with me in the weeks that followed.

And what followed was beyond what I could ever have imagined. Sunday morning, Tony went to the petrol station and there on the front page of the *SST* was a mammoth photo of our family, together with my question to Helen Clark. The paper was filled with story after story about the factors in New Zealand society that had pushed me to snap on that April afternoon. Within hours, the phone was ringing, talkback radio debate was firing and the roller-coaster had begun.

The [NEW] Parent CODE

From anonymous phone calls of 'You go girl – we're in the same boat as you!' to Gary McCormick and Linda Clark, people from north and south were phoning their support. National and ACT politicians also phoned to discuss the issues I had raised.

Very quickly I realised that this wasn't about Tony and Marilynn of Waihi, but rather was about a huge number of Kiwis out there who were struggling with the same issues. Every journalist who approached me had a personal story to share before the formal interview. It appeared that everyone knew the average New Zealand family was struggling, but we were all pretending we didn't. People were almost apologetic when they admitted their own salary – $50,000, $100,000 or even $200,000 more than we were bringing in, but then those people lived in the city and paid more than triple our mortgage, had higher travel expenses and so on.

A professional budgeter was brought to my home. She rubbed her hands in delight at being able to work with a family bringing in such a high salary – most of her clients earned far less. A few hours later, she left in defeat. No, we were not doing okay. We were going downhill at a rate of around $150 per week. And that didn't count debts already accrued.

The following week, I was flown to the Beehive to meet with the Minister of Social Development, Steve Maharey, and the Leader of the Opposition, Don Brash. My biggest concern initially was flying (particularly into Wellington airport) and then, as I walked into the Beehive, memories flashed back of my last visit. It was 2000, the All Blacks had just lost to Australia 'in overtime', and the quality of the referee's watch was called into question. The after-match function was held at the Beehive. As I wandered around, I started having contractions that got increasingly severe. While it turned out to be a false alarm – Lachy was born a week later – it didn't make for pleasant memories.

My first sign of nervousness about the meetings came when I entered Mr Maharey's office and my stomach did a bit of a flip-flop. I'd heard him talk about me to Linda Clark and I'd already decided that I wouldn't like him or what he might have to say. He wouldn't let any journalist come to the interview and when we sat down to chat (with two IRD experts, a secretary and a WINZ worker) the look in his eyes told me that he thought as little of me as I did of him. He had made presumptions about me, as I had about him.

What ensued, however, was the chat that I had originally sought with the Prime Minister. He knew the pressure that New Zealand families were under, and assured me that the upcoming Budget would be addressing this issue. He pointed out an inaccuracy in my original letter and explained the plan his party had for New Zealand.

The plan involved three phases: first to improve the economic circumstances of our nation (thereby reducing unemployment); secondly to improve the lifestyle of those who depend on welfare and those on lower incomes; and, finally the 2004 Budget would address middle New Zealanders – the ones who pay lots of tax yet see very little in return. It made sense to me. Most important, this man appeared to give a damn about the country.

Following this meeting, I went to meet Don Brash who didn't say much except that Labour was doing it all wrong, National would do it better, but National hadn't made any policy decisions yet. What *wasn't* reported, and somewhat embarrassing for me, was that Madeline (who had travelled with me) had completely lost it by this stage of the day and I had to sit there breastfeeding. Dr Brash was very understanding but it was an experience I would rather have done without.

I had gone to Parliament believing National would have the answers, only to come away believing Labour was going to be the party to exact societal change.

I don't believe in the subsequent Budget that Labour has got it all right, but I haven't seen any other party come close to addressing the issues involved.

On my return flight, I felt as though a weight had been lifted from my shoulders. I had received the answers I sought and had a little more understanding about the decisions politicians were making on my behalf (whether I liked them or not).

It was quite liberating. The journalists from the SST had shown in their investigations that this was a real problem. The budgeter had admitted defeat and left saying that I needed to get a job, but not during the daylight hours because I wouldn't be able to afford childcare. The letters, cards and phone calls from Kiwis around the country confirmed that this wasn't my problem, something *I* was doing wrong.

Let me be quite honest, however, about the downsides of putting your views on the line. In the middle of the roller-coaster of media attention I was accused of all sorts of things – from being a political plant, to being an abuser of the poor. Indeed, I was gob-smacked that after my meeting with Steve Maharey he later stood up in Parliament and accused my family of being ACT affiliates. He said that either Tony or I may be standing in the next election as a member of the ACT party. I found his comments both personally insulting and ironic – I had only considered entering the political arena after my meeting with him.

There was a portion of society that was unable to view the investigations from a distance. To some people I was a failure to my children, a spoilt brat or someone who had no handle on reality. These people represented only a small part of a group who continue to put me through an emotional wringer with their personal abuse of both me and my family.

In reality, however, not one of these people represents the group for whom my letter was relevant.

Letter Writer to Book Writer

How does one get from writing a letter to the Prime Minister about the realities of the New Zealand family to writing a book about parenting?

To understand this, I'd like to step back into pre-letter times. I have four children, the first of whom I became pregnant with at 21. The biological father has not seen him since he was one, and has drifted well into the background. I met husband Tony and married him at 25, and we had a further three children in quick succession. Tony and I both have a fundamental belief in 'family first' and want the best for our children. We moved from Wellington to the small town of Waihi for the cheaper lifestyle.

We both fully believe in children's natural capabilities and that we need to provide our children with the best environment we can in order for them to flourish into happy, intelligent and creative adults. I have read everything I could get my hands on about child development, from Gardner to Montessori to Steiner to Piaget. I have devoured the contents of newspapers and Internet sites, with their articles on child rearing.

All the while, many people I met treated me as some kind of societal anomaly (my goodness – four children – who would do that?) and as someone who had limited intellectual capabilities.

I began to sift through all of this information and to form my own conclusions about child rearing. The information I was getting everywhere reinforced a single message: *I was a parental failure.*

It is a small step for me from admitting and coming under scrutiny for my financial failures to admitting my parental ones. My letter to the Prime Minister received so much support because so many other parents were feeling like failures. It is not just about finances, it is about many areas to do with parenting – breastfeeding, childcare, schooling, NCEA and developing intelligence. The messages come so fast and hard for parents that we've failed before we've even begun.

Knowing that going back to work was a necessity for me, Tony and I had long conversations about what work I could take on. We talked about entering politics, going back teaching or stacking shelves at the local supermarket. In all our discussions, however, we couldn't get away from the fact that I was feeling the pressure suffered by many parents and their children today. I continue to feel very strongly about the lack of confidence we have in ourselves; I feel the pressure experienced by little children growing up, needing to belong to their family and to have a chance to develop their full potential when they enter society.

My own experiences have been incredibly varied – I've been a solo mum on the DPB, a full-time working mum, a full-time stay-at-home mum. I have also taken on part-time and temporary work at various times through the years – including teaching (from five- to 18-year-olds); working at a youth centre; going to high schools educating students about self-esteem, drugs, alcohol and sex; and doing the odd bit of writing. I've experienced what it is like when a male decides he wants nothing to do with his child, and I've experienced what it is like when a man walks by your side in the parenting journey.

I've experienced the numbness of long-term post-natal depression, and I've experienced the anxiety that comes with the parenting journey, that makes me second-guess myself every step of the way.

A book provides a medium for discussing the issues facing so many parents today. A book is an excellent forum for opening up discussion about the real world of parenting, not some ideal that makes sense to very few people.

This book is about looking objectively at the messages we are being fed and drawing conclusions based on *our* reality, not those of a researcher or an expert with the next brilliant idea for nurturing the next generation.

What makes my view somewhat different from these is that I am from Generation X (born 1965–1975), the generation raised with the belief that everyone could do it for themselves. I was raised during the years where the divorce rate doubled. While my own parents remained married, I witnessed the devastating effects of the breakdown of a family on some of my closest friends, some of whom are still trying to heal today. I am from the first generation of New Zealanders to enter family life with student debt hanging over our heads. With $40,000 still owing on my student loan, I know that with whatever money I earn, I will pay my taxes and then add another 10 per cent towards my loan repayment. The student loan scheme came into force the year I entered Palmerston North College of Education – 1992. I didn't fully understand the implications then, but I certainly do now. When discussions about the tax rate come up, we always have to remember that we – the Gen-Xers – are paying another ten cents in every dollar.

We are the generation that has been raised in two-income families, and are often labelled 'latchkey' children – meaning that we had less contact with our parents and are more reliant on our peers for emotional support. We grew up with technology and all around us materialism was the mantra of the day. We were raised to be independent and to question authority, just as the adults were beginning to do as we grew up.

Now we are having children and we see the pitfalls of a self-indulgent, dog-eat-dog world. We are the living result of a nation whose religion is independence. We entered a society that allowed Baby Boomers (born

1946–1964) to have a supported family, free education and health care, and these very same people took these things away from us in the name of independence and freedom. The Baby Boomers still stand in Parliament – with or without children – and continue to preside over a nation that does nothing for Generation X or their children. The Baby Boomers with children do not have a student loan hanging over their heads.

The Baby Boomers' children are the so-called Y generation (born 1976–1981), or the 'echo-boomer' generation. We shall talk about this phenomenon in greater detail later, but for now we need to introduce the latest generation: Generation Xtra, (my publisher Finlay Macdonald must be attributed with creating this label) the children of the Xers. We are going to form a new parent code, based on *our* reality, which is very different than the one we have been fed.

With four children, my objective is to share with you that which I have found most useful. I aim to cut through all the crap – and there is a lot – and find something we can use rather than something we can beat ourselves up with.

My first question upon writing this book was to ask myself what I had in common with you, the reader. For days I pondered and finally came to the conclusion that the only thing that we have in common is the ability to say: '*I am a parent.*' Beyond this, the scope for individuality is huge: you may be a solo parent; a gay parent; a heterosexual parent; an adoptive parent; a parent with one child or seven children; your income could be $20,000, $200,000 or $2,000,000; you could stay at home all day, every day with your children, or you could work seven days a week.

Such a broad definition didn't really help me much. I had to break it down, and I have made three assumptions about you:

1. You give a damn about your child or children.

2. You are suffering from information overload and/or guilt.

3. You need a new and real perspective of parenting that works for you, rather than an ideal you do not relate to.

This is the perspective on which this book is founded.

I have been to hell and back in trying to get everything 'right' for my children. The problem was that the 'right' kept changing (this happens in education circles, too). I've talked to numerous parents, I've explored the theorists and I've experienced the reality of the pressure that parents face in their parenting role.

Before we go any further I'd like to make one thing clear: in writing that letter to Helen Clark, I was placed in a nice little box with a label that verged, for some people, on sainthood. Nothing could be further from the truth. I get grumpy at my kids, I have days where I wish I could run away and never return, and I have dreams of what life will be like when I can go to the toilet in peace.

I am no longer idealistic about parenthood; you will not find any nice, cushy, fluffy feelings or birthday party ideas in this book. I don't have all the answers. I merely present some questions, some possible solutions and voice my personal experiences as well as those of a number of mums and dads who gave their time to contribute to this book.

I have no hidden agenda; I have no desire to turn you into a parental saint or to tell you what you should and shouldn't be doing. My only concern is to get real about this parenting thing and to sort through all the information to find that which will be truly useful to us in our role. I will look at the 12 parent 'codes' currently being presented to us; render them obsolete for our purposes; and propose 12 *new* codes based on our society as it is today.

I welcome you to the journey of parenthood: the highs, the lows and the bits in between. But let's start at the most important place: exploding the ideal of perfection.

ACKNOWLEDGEMENTS

As with any book, there are a number of people who have helped shape its outcome and deserve to be thanked for their varied roles.

All things start with parents, and so it is with me. Through the years I know I haven't been the easiest daughter but both of my parents have shaped my personality and view on life in powerful ways. Mum taught me that it is okay to be different and that I need not conform to other people's expectations. My Dad taught me to always question, to have my own mind and to think deeply. To both of them - thank you.

Thank you to Dianne Northcott, who proves beyond a doubt that one teacher, can make a difference in a student's life.

Thank you to Mark and Sharon Samson, Damon, and Georgia and Jacob for their friendship.

Thank you to Donna Chisholm, for believing in and supporting me.

Thank you to Sally, who is an angel.

Thank you to my sister Brenda, who never doubted me. Thank you to my brother Craig.

Thank you to my in-laws, Tony and Marg Gilbert for your unconditional acceptance of me into your family.

Thank you to Murray – one of life's gentlemen.

Thanks must also be made to my agent Michael Gifkins for his reflection and comments of the work in progress as well as keeping me strong when times were tough.

Thank you to Penguin Books, including commissioning editor Finlay Macdonald who helped me through the entire process and Alison Brook who had the hard job of going through my work with a fine-toothed comb and yet somehow always remained positive and encouraging.

Thank you to those people, many of whom I have never met, who supported our family with letters and phone calls. It was your belief in what I did that enabled this book to be written.

Finally, thank you to Tony who taught me to laugh. He is in every way a husband with whom I couldn't do without. And to my four wonderful children, Kalym, Lachlan, Malachy and Madeline, who have taught me so much about the world and who make me want to push myself further than I ever dreamed possible.

Code ONE

THE OLD CODE: Perfectionism

Do you have a firm idea of how your home should look, how your body should be shaped, what dinners you should be serving and how your child should be a combination Mozart, Einstein, Picasso and Pitt?

Ah, yes, perfection in life. It's the way life is meant to be. Just go to your local bookstore; wander through to the self-help section and then venture to the business section. When you've done that, perhaps take a walk to the spirituality section. Within these three sections of the store, you will have found literally hundreds of books offering ways to improve your life. Each one has its own secret. Each one promises to tell you how you can have more, do more and be more.

Have you picked up any magazines lately? You'll find plenty to highlight your imperfections.

Have you watched television lately? You'll be getting the same message, I'm sure.

A Long Way from Perfect . . .

Sit down for a moment and let your imagination conjure up a vision of parenthood so pure and perfect that you are immediately soothed into a world where the birds sing and time moves with slow perfection.

Love

Picture man and woman in love and untouchable. She has beautiful long flowing hair with luscious red lips. He arrives on a white horse, a silver cape draped across his shoulder. They are soulmates, destined to be together across time and space.

✷ REALITY CHECK

Knights on white horses and perfect women should be saved for childhood fairy tales. The only perfect couple was Tom Cruise and Nicole Kidman, and they broke up.

Pregnancy

The couple share magic times and make perfect love on a summer's evening beneath the stars. As they reach a simultaneous orgasm their souls entwine and, unbeknown to them both, their lovemaking produces the beginnings of a foetus.

Six weeks later, the woman is glowing. She has a faint inkling that she may be carrying a baby and dances off to the doctor for confirmation. She is overwhelmed with happiness and returns to the man of her dreams to share her news. He is delighted. He holds her tight, promises to look after her, and sets about making plans to provide for his love and his soon-to-be prodigy.

With each passing day, the woman swells. Her breasts enlarge, her lips enlarge and she begins to feel more like a woman. The baby is fulfilling a part of her she never knew existed. She makes endless plans for Baby's room, his or her life, the type of parent she will be and what the birth will be like. She reads books about birth, realises the power of mind over body and knows that birth is a beautiful, natural experience. She exercises and mentally prepares for the awesome experience ahead.

✳ REALITY CHECK

A woman suspects she is pregnant after feeling faint and puking on a regular basis. She confirms it by peeing on a stick, panics about what to do about her career, and whether she can mentally, physically, emotionally and financially handle having a baby.

If she continues with the pregnancy she learns that she may suffer from any or all of the following:

* hair loss and hair gain (both in the wrong places)
* obsessive-compulsive disorder
* backache
* deteriorating eyesight
* sore breasts
* blood-pressure problems (high or low, it's still awful)
* morning sickness (which can be any time of the day or all day, every day)
* mood swings
* swelling (legs, hands, feet – you name it)
* stretch marks

There's a lot more to mention, but we don't want to get ourselves too depressed.

Birth

Some eight months later, with a slight gasp of discomfort, Baby comes out, charming and beautiful. The little darling looks at Mum and smiles. Dad watches in wonder.

✳ REALITY CHECK

Imagine a white hot rod being shoved up you know where, and we can begin to fathom the pain involved. Birth is having your insides ripped out, and the final product is doused in blood and white vernix. Quite likely it resembles a small ape that only Mum and Dad can truly appreciate (except for our children – they were gorgeous, weren't they?)

Mum finds it hard to nurture babe after birth because the contractions do not stop following delivery – only after the placenta passes, but no one bothers to tell the pregnant woman this vital piece of information.

Breastfeeding

The new mum brings her babe to her swelled and perfect breast where it immediately latches on for its first feed. It is a beautiful experience that bonds Mum and baby instantly. The beauty will continue for months to come.

✳ REALITY CHECK

Many women find breastfeeding (particularly the first child) damn near impossible. Baby seems to resist, Mum can't work out which way to hold her baby.

A nurse or midwife shoves breast and babe's mouth around until the connection is made. It's much easier after the first, but the nipple pain is still like small needles pricking you, no matter how many babies you have and this can last for up to a week. Also, every time you feed (bottle or breast) for a week or so after delivery you have 'after pains', which basically means contractions reminiscent of labour. These get worse and last longer with each subsequent baby. Of course, don't forget the blisters that may form. Any woman unfortunate enough to get mastitis will learn about a whole new form of pain.

Home

They go home and the little babe rests dearly in her bed, while her parents can't believe their good fortune.

✳ REALITY CHECK

Newborn infants are not biologically made to sleep for long periods of time. In fact, feeding every two to three hours is *normal*. It can be easy to get lulled into a false sense of security because the baby can sleep so much in the first few days. Sleep patterns continue to change, and a normal pattern of sleep can be disrupted by sickness, teething, restlessness or anything else that may unsettle them.

The first poo to come from the dear little bottom is thick, tar-like meconium that you have to almost scrape off.

Growing up

Baby grows up, of course, but life remains perfect. She is incredibly talented, she helps around the home, she is caring and gentle, and she is of perfect disposition. She does what she is told, she loves school and brings constant light in her childhood years to her ever-proud, adoring and patient parents.

✳ REALITY CHECK

The growing child is her own individual person. She has her own likes and dislikes. She is learning her own boundaries, and the boundaries you have set up. She wants to test your love. She is emotionally immature, and gets upset and cries over things you think are not worth it. She scribbles on the walls and paints her own body for fun. She resists instruction but will sometimes listen if it is done in a respectful and preferably fun way – or if you threaten her with consequences.

Adolescence

When she hits adolescence, what an adult emerges! She is confident, successful, intelligent and goes on to have a career as a volunteer doctor in Africa, while in the evenings she finds a cure for cancer and Aids. She is her parents' pride and joy, their greatest ideal.

✳ REALITY CHECK

The hormones hit hard and fast in adolescence so that even she does not understand her changing emotions and body. She is seeking to distance herself from you and to form her own place in the world. The harder you resist her growing, the further she'll wander. She can hate you as much as she needs your love. She sleeps often, because this is what her body needs (not because she's lazy). She spends hours staring into space doing nothing. She moves into adulthood overly idealistic and often confused.

My Story

I am not quite sure how I expected life to be with children. I remember dreams of beauty and softness, of feeling more complete, more of a woman, with little darlings attached to my skirt. I was certainly idealistic and I think that in order to venture on the parenting road, this idealism is necessary – for who would choose this path knowing how difficult it really is? The reality is far more real and raw than I had ever thought possible.

The realities involved in the parenting journey were something that I denied, denied and further denied until my first child was around six months old, when the truth came crashing down around my ears. Sleep deprivation, solo-motherhood, financial stress and isolation all culminated into what was later diagnosed as post-natal depression. I crashed. Hard.

Now, almost nine years later, I've found my partner. Not only that, I've even chosen to have another three children. Just after my 29th birthday I had my fourth child – a girl, Madeline. I no longer have great ideals about how my life or my children should be. I don't plan as much as I used to. Then again, I don't stress nearly as much, or worry about things that would have once brought me to the brink of insanity. Our McLachlan-Gilbert world is rarely still. One person's crisis ends, to be followed by the next person's. Our house seems in a permanent state of disarray, no matter how many times I clean or try and teach my children to pick up after themselves. It's a lifestyle I wouldn't recommend to everyone, but it is one I adore. Yes, there are things I'd change, but for the most part I consider myself damn lucky.

THE NEW CODE: Realism

Let's put the ideal of perfection in the bin
labelled 'Obsolete Ideals' where it deserves
to be. Why? Because it only leads us to feelings
of failure and guilt – for, who has the perfect
life? I don't, that's for sure.

We feel anxious and guilty because we receive constant messages
that if we haven't got the perfect life *we are doing something wrong.* We
should have the perfect life – this is what the Baby Boomers have, and
they set the systems in place so that we could have it all, without
having to fight for it. Now that we Generation Xers are convinced of
this, there are many individuals and businesses out there to lure us
into spending big money to achieve this perfection. It's a nasty, vicious

cycle that needs to be stopped. Now. It is making us miserable.

Until around four years ago, I was hooked on the perfection treadmill. And because of this I could never, ever be happy with my life, my family, my home or myself. As this is a parenting book, I shall focus only on our expectation of perfection as it relates to us as parents, and to our children.

Perfect Parents

First, let's look at ourselves. I have a story to share with you. It is one that liberated me (and I don't use that term lightly) from trying to be the perfect parent, filled with god-like qualities.

When I was living in suburban Wellington, I would observe other mums taking their children to the kindergarten and admire them. They always seemed so in control. Their hair was always perfect, their clothes were perfect, and their cars were perfect. I always felt so inadequate next to them. I was pregnant with child number three, and was barely coping with life. My four-year-old was running me ragged and my six-month-old seemed to scream constantly. My husband and I, buckling under financial pressures and coping with two young children and another on the way, seemed to argue all the time. I envied the other women around me – until one day I was invited to one of their get-togethers. It's not normally my cup of tea, but I thought the experience would be good for me – an opportunity to chat with other women who shared the common experience of motherhood. While our children played, the women chatted. I was so enormously shocked by the conversation that I heard, I came away realising how normal I was. From that day forth, I have never again looked at another woman with envy or jealousy, thinking they have it all. They don't.

What I learned that day from these normal women in middle-income New Zealand, who seemed to be so in control and content, was that they were, in fact, miserable. They were just like everybody else, trying to do the best they could, believing that staying at home with their children was the right thing to do. The problem was, they weren't coping. In this group of women, each had their own way of coping with their lifestyle.

Some were on anti-depressant medication. All joked about how they watched the clock every day until the big hand was on the 12 and the little hand on the five so that they could have their first drink of the day. Some joked that they often couldn't make it this long. Another was having an affair with her husband's work partner. Another woman was having an affair with two different men. Another smoked marijuana every evening, as it was the only thing that helped her relax.

As if all this wasn't enough, these women had, in my observation, ultimately lost faith in themselves. They didn't allow themselves to think too deeply about anything, either personal or societal.

Did I catch these women on a bad day? Were they a minority experiencing the frustration and pain of mothering? In the end, it doesn't matter because I watched them, and I listened to them and I came away a free woman: *perfection does not exist.*

The idea of perfection actually goes against our very human nature, which is a dichotomy of good and bad. We are not meant to be happy all day, every day. We are not meant to have an easy life-road. We are not meant to experience only good. Think about it logically – how would you know what your limits are, how much would you push yourself emotionally, physically, intellectually, and spiritually if everything was always positive and good? There would be no point in seeking answers or in challenging ourselves, because perfection would always exist. How insanely boring. If you had nothing to compare the good times with, then you wouldn't appreciate them when they came along.

Through the ages, great thinkers, philosophers, psychologists and scientists have battled with life's mixture of good and bad. Each school of thought has provided answers that suited their purposes – whether it was becoming an 'integrated' person as psychology wants you to, or becoming 'born-again' as Christianity wants you to, or losing yourself completely by realising your godliness and becoming an enlightened human as the Buddha did.

Forget it all. You don't need to live in the bush or be persecuted for your beliefs, or spend years considering life's dichotomy. You only need to become a parent. Parenting is the greatest, most practical, living example of dichotomy.

The good

On the one hand, parenting is a powerful, beautiful experience. It reaches into your very depths and finds strength and love that is so giving and patient that you would be forgiven for thinking that you were the only person to have ever felt it.

My children are alive and functioning well today because of Tony and me. I carried them in my womb. We fed, clothed and sheltered them. We played with them, created with them and dreamed with them. This exhilarates me. It fills me with pride and peace, knowing that I have birthed and nurtured the young and defenceless. There is something very natural, very worldly about this experience. It makes me appreciate the small, everyday things that I would have otherwise ignored. It has made me realise that intellectualism is not enough, it cannot lead to complete satisfaction in life because it is disconnected and somewhat unreal.

It is the slow-moving and natural life that allows children to unfold naturally.

Indeed, there are times when I feel pure and complete, where all those positive qualities have a place to grow – things like unconditional love, compassion, forgiveness, truth, gentleness and hope.

Parenting, in this sense, is an incredibly *life-giving* experience.

The bad

On the other hand, parenting can be a stagnant life. This is the raw, negative emotion that drives me to want to close the door on their screams and to crawl under a rock and hide forever. There is no escape, no relief and its power rips me. In this place I grieve for the person I once was and the freedom I once held.

Here, it is easy to rest miserable, unwilling to make changes. It is dull and sucks the life from the parent and those around him or her. It is easy to get stuck in an idea about how life should be, so that other people become an intrusion if they enter this world. The home becomes the ultimate focus and, because of this, personal expression becomes almost obsolete. It is filled with bitterness and resentment – towards children, partner or society.

It represents the ugly – impatience, grumpiness, stress, selfishness and boredom.

This flip side is the *life-suffocating* experience.

The merging

This confrontation between the good and bad sides of the parenting experience requires patience. It takes time to accept the good and the bad as existing side by side.

It continues to amaze me that each day, indeed each hour, I can be taken for a ride that is so high and awesome in one moment and then so low and dark the next.

Parenting is the most life-giving and life-suffocating experience there is.

Perfect Children

It is not just perfection in ourselves that we expect, but in our children also. This expectation breeds competitiveness between parents and makes us put undue pressure on our children.

I always listen with absolute fascination when other parents tell me stories about the perfection of their children. There are, according to stories I've heard, parents out there who have children that sleep through the night from birth, who never argue or question what Mum or Dad says, who were never a problem feeding or toilet training, and who as teenagers never brought a furrowed brow of concern to their parents' faces. If these stories are true (and I seriously doubt it) I say wonderful, great. And then I say: it's a fluke. Go and have a second, and if you've already done that, have a third. If you've done that, then I don't mean to offend you, but I don't believe you. Or maybe I'm just insanely jealous.

In my experience as a mother, a teacher and as a friend to other parents I have *never* come across the perfect child. Ever. By perfect, I mean the conforming type, the one who does things by the book, who is always predictable and nice. Experience tells me that children are just not that simple. Children are curious and adventurous creatures who naturally push boundaries, whatever their age. It helps them understand where they belong and what societal norms exist around them. One child may thrive on cuddles and love while another thrives on their parents' precious time alone. Whatever expectations or ideals a parent holds, these are exactly the expectations and ideals that the child will then challenge.

> *I always had it in the back of my mind that my son would be wearing knickers by the age of two. As his second birthday came closer and closer I became more anxious as he showed absolutely no interest in going anywhere near the toilet. A month before he was two, I put him in knickers and every day he refused to use the toilet. He would always just go in his knickers. I got more and more desperate – I tried everything: showing him pictures of children going to the toilet, praising him, a reward system – nothing worked. He just wouldn't use the toilet. I found myself getting angry with him, like he was doing it just to annoy me. One day I cried in utter frustration. Sitting on the bathroom floor and looking at the confusion on his face I wondered what the hell I was doing. Why I was putting us both through this? I gave up and waited. He was over three when he was finally toilet trained, but it involved very little stress or heartache.*
>
> *Vicky*

Children have their own path to follow and will do so in their own time. The more they feel rushed and pressured, the more their resistance mounts. Their resistance is either overt: raging temper tantrums, or covert: dragging their heels and sulking. If you are in a rush and need to get somewhere, this is the time when a child will rebel. If you are worried that they need to be on their best behaviour to impress the other parents at a party, this will be the time they throw their biggest tantrum.

Eventually, the futility of it all begins to make sense. When I back off and let my children be whomever they want to be (and this doesn't mean being verbally or physically violent) they behave like gems.

Perfection = Big business

Creating the ideal of perfect children is a huge industry. This ideal is a massive play on the guilt and inadequacy we are feeling. If our child is not perfect, it is our fault. This line of thinking brings us to the point of feeling unhappy with our own children. If they come second in an exam, why didn't they come first? We are developing an expectation of perfection – in sports, music, science, art, dance, math, English, behaviour, demeanour, looks and clothing.

From the perspective of the child, the past couple of decades have been very exciting. Children *are* filled with potential – not simply waiting for maturity before they can learn and understand. Children are now being credited with far more potential than they were in the past, and are indeed achieving (usually academically) in ways that were a rarity in the past.

The potential of the child, however, has been twisted and distorted so that if a child acts like a child and plays up or throws a temper tantrum parents are hooked into believing that their child is abnormal because he or she is less than perfect.

The New Disease: Guilt

While it is nice to hold some fairy-tale ideal in our heads, and to aim for the best, the expectation of perfection actually makes us sick with a disease that saps our energy, leaves a pit of emptiness in our stomachs and ultimately makes us worse parents.

The disease? Why, it is guilt.

As I sit down to write about the guilt epidemic, I have just left my three children at a local childcare centre. As we pulled up the driveway, three-year-old Lachy decided that he didn't want to go. Two-year-old Malachy joined in the chant and within minutes I had a near riot on my hands. My only saving grace was one-year-old Madeline who was bouncing up and down, eager to get inside and start her play.

It took around 20 minutes to leave the boys behind. We had to get shoes off, lunchboxes in the fridge, bags in a cubbyhole and a name tag each. That was before we even got inside the door. With protests all the way, I managed to get them into the centre. Malachy, seeing the cars and tracks set up, got all excited and began to play. There was no such appeasement for Lachy, however. I left him screaming at me. 'I don't want to go to kindy,' his face red with anger and pain, and his eyes hating me.

It's the way it has to be in our world at the moment. Mummy has to work, Daddy has to work and so Lachy has to go to kindy. *I* know why it has to be done but he doesn't. He just wants to stay at home with his mum, even though I know he'll get bored and nag me the entire time. So here I am, writing about parental guilt, ravaged with guilt myself.

Guilt. The very word is onomatopoeic in its nature. Go on and say it aloud. Feel the heaviness about the heart that it produces. Feel your shoulders automatically slump.

This is the anchor that almost every parent I know carries with them, wherever they may go, whatever they may do. We are riddled with this disease and everywhere we look, society seems to reinforce our feelings.

The disease

Let's begin by trying to understand this disease. The DSM-IV (the dictionary of mental illness) doesn't diagnose guilt as a specific disease (perhaps this will come in DSM-V) but it does give plenty of examples of psychiatric illnesses where excessive and inappropriate guilt are contributing factors to mental illness.

Although the DSM-IV can't help, the trusty dictionary can:

'Guilt *n.* fact or state of having done wrong; remorse for wrongdoing.'

So now we begin to get a clearer picture: parents are stuck in a state of believing they have done wrong. Failed. See what comes of idealising our parenting experience and our children?

And *why* do we feel guilty? Because other people keep ramming our failure down our throats!

Raising our children in guilt is a self-defeating, self-absorbed approach to parenting that doesn't benefit anyone, especially our children. It leads to pendulum parenting, where a parent is over-indulgent one moment and not around the next. It leads parents to be too lenient towards their children, because they feel guilty for saying no to them. It makes parents spend more money on their child than is ever necessary.

Too much guilt ultimately leads to ineffective parenting because the parent is always overanxious and frustrated.

The guilt pill

You are a better parent than you think you are!

Read it, say it and believe it.

The time has come for us as parents to take a stand and to acknowledge that we are doing the best damn job that we can. We are forging our own path in a society where staying at home with children is rarely an option. Even if it is, nothing has prepared us for the isolation of being in a suburban home with limited conversation where money dictates choices.

The fact that you're reading this book shows that you already care about your child and his or her well-being. You probably already have some sort of home/work balance because if you were working 12 hours a day, seven days a week, you wouldn't have time to read this book.

There are, of course, times when our guilt is justified. When we do something or say something to our child that we regret. When this happens, go and apologise to them and then move on. Don't use it to beat yourself up over the next 20 years so that when your child leaves their marriage you can say it is your fault because of something you did to them when they were nine. Life doesn't work that way. It is okay to have regrets, to wistfully look back at another time or another place, but if that leads you to thinking you have failed your child, you are on the wrong track.

The biggest question I have to ask myself is: 'What is really important to me? What do I truly want ?' i.e. Is it getting jobs done quickly or seeing that my children are happy? I've found that on several occasions I've managed to get a lot of jobs done in one day, but I'm not happy because of it. This is because I know my children have not had a happy or fun day. There's been limited playing and they've been dragged from one place to the next. After I put my children to bed I don't say, 'Yay, I got all my jobs done.' Instead I say, 'What a terrible day, there's been nothing in it for the girls.' Why, then, do I keep trying to get my jobs done in a hurry?

I know that quite often I can get the job done and keep my children happy if I just slow down and get rid of those deadlines that have been cemented in my mind from years of schooling and work. So what if they wear crumpled trousers, live in an untidy home, and arrive at daycare with a far less than perfect hairstyle?

Britta

We love our children. We spend time with our children. We cuddle and sing and read with our children.

Let's look at all the positives of what we are doing and cure ourselves of this guilt that is based on the belief that someone else is doing it so much better.

Identify what it is you're feeling guilty about and free yourself. We are not the wrong age, in the wrong place, or doing the wrong thing. We do not have to justify our choices to other people. We each make our own individual choices based on our individual experiences in the best way we can. And that's enough.

Code TWO

THE OLD CODE: Dependency

We live in an information society. We have information at our fingertips. We are being bombarded almost daily with new information on everything from health to money to happiness.

The advice we are given about being a parent and what is best for our children changes regularly. This is exactly what makes our guilty feelings thrive. Another study, another thing we've done wrong.

There are many people offering many different views about children and what is best for them. I confess that in the past I have been one of the worst people I know for relying on information I've learned. Nothing wrong with this, in itself, but it meant that at times I became fixated on how my home or children or life should be. I could never match up to the ideal presented in whichever study or theory I was looking at and the next thing I knew, I was failing again. I've been through so many theories, I feel sorry for my children.

Now I have found there is no one idea I look at and think: that's it, that is the perfect idea – if I follow this idea I will never again feel guilty because I've done all the right things and my children will be perfectly happy and achieving great things.

The Parent Breakdown

Once upon a time parents were given credit for knowing how to parent. Mum had her role and Dad had his. Dad often worked at home, or at least near the home and would come home at lunchtime for a warm meal. Mum looked after the home and the kids. Communities were actual communities, as opposed to individuals living side by side. Let's not idealise it at all, but there appears to have been a lot of support around. Mum raised the kids as best as she could, and asked for advice when she needed it, but was pretty much left alone to do her thing.

Then the Industrial Revolution struck. Individual families (rather than extended families) moved up and out of the rural communities into urban centres. Dad was out of the house most of the day while Mum was left to raise the kids in a much smaller and more lonely environment.

Side by side with the Industrial Revolution came the rise of the medicine man and government involvement in education. In the medical arena, women slowly but surely began to lose control of the pregnancy and birthing process. These became medical conditions to be dealt with by medical experts. In a few short decades, birth became hospital-focussed with a woman's legs strapped to stirrups, her pubic hair shaved and procedures like episiotomies routinely performed. The education of children changed so that it became a government initiative, and children were taught what the government thought they needed to learn.

There were obvious positives to such initiatives. People became more aware of the need for hygiene, for example. Illnesses that once killed became manageable and, in many cases, avoidable. Education for all meant that everyone had the opportunity to learn how to read and write, making for a more equitable society.

The negatives of such initiatives, however, meant that parents slowly but surely began to lose control over their own children. More and more choices were taken away. By the 1950s parents were fed an ideal of Mum at home with the kids (yet not able to educate or nurse them) while Dad went out to work with his briefcase and a smile. The economy was running hot and government policy supported the family. The children of that generation, the Baby Boomers, were raised in a stable, supportive society – a society they subsequently rebelled against in the years to come. But mothers were finding it all beyond their capabilities. They needed advice – and lots of it.

Doctor Frederick Truby King

One of New Zealand's biggest parenting 'experts' was Doctor Frederick Truby King, the man behind the Plunket movement. Many people look back with pride on the fact that our small corner of the world produced one of the biggest influences in child rearing of the early 1900s.

Plunket was founded in 1907 as an organisation set-up by women, for women. Its success as a voluntary organisation in supporting mothers and children can not be underestimated or over-appreciated. Truby King – for all his positive beliefs in things like breastfeeding and hygiene – was a product of his time. A man with a medical background, he was firm in his views: he believed that women were ignorant of the correct methods of child rearing, and were therefore in need of education.

This doctor was adamant that there was only one way to raise children, and that involved using a clock. Feeding and sleeping by the parental schedule meant that little babes would turn into perfect and obedient children. If the babe cried – *ignore them*, he taught. Such crying was good for the baby – it strengthened their lungs and fostered their independence.

And sleeping? Well, that was simple too. Place them on their stomach.

And what of nurturing? Be sure not to indulge Baby by actually cuddling or kissing them. Such behaviour would make the child weak and dependent later in life. If nurturing involved playing, a parent was to make sure that they did no such thing before the age of six months. Such young babies didn't need such stimulation – in fact, it was bad for them.

His techniques were so rigid that many women felt intimidated and refused to rely on their own intuition for fear of being a bad mother.

There were some real problems with our Doctor King. The number of cot deaths has significantly decreased since we learned that babies should sleep on their backs. We've learned that no child can be spoiled with affection. We've learned that even the youngest child needs stimulation and play.

It wasn't until the 1970s that Plunket began to shift its philosophy towards one involving a partnership with the mother.

Doctor Benjamin Spock

Doctor King maintained world status as a parenting expert until the middle of the 1960s. Then in came Doctor Spock, who took a firm footing internationally about how to look after and raise children. His *Pocket Book of Baby and Childcare*, first published in 1946, had reached its 150th printing by 1965, with more than 16 million copies sold.

We could sit here in the 21st century and laugh at Doctor Spock's advice. Surely we have much more knowledge now than he did in the 1940s and 50s about how to raise children? A quick flip through his book, however, shows his underlying philosophy is just as important today as it was almost 60 years ago. He addresses the needs of women, parental doubts and fears and the individuality of children. He makes a case for the unnaturalness of separating baby and mother from birth, no small feat in an era when the medical profession had gained super-human status. It is a down to earth and highly practical book that was once second only to the Bible for every family to read and understand. Life is a lot simpler when there is just one book of such information.

But even Spock brought problems for women. His views were in almost complete opposition to King's. Maternal instinct was natural and *expected* – from the first few minutes of life. Medical experts were to watch with care to make sure Mum was feeling nice, comfy feelings.

Mums had to do everything, for the baby was dependent solely upon her – there was very little for Dad to do.

Spock's success provided the springboard for umpteen books about child development and parenting. Information became more and more specific. Feeding a babe now no longer requires a chapter outlining the options and possible solutions – it requires several books about nutrition, foods that are good for the brain, how to pack a school lunch, what to cook for dinner, how many meals a child should be eating, and let's not forget the books about how to be a successful breastfeeder or bottle feeder.

This knowledge-specific approach to child rearing is raising the anxiety levels of today's parents. One small piece of research can quickly become the next new fad, and expert after expert arrives on the scene to teach parents how to raise better, happier and brighter children. There would be nothing wrong with this, except that there are so many different approaches and so much contradictory advice that parents end up confused and disappointed, and feeling like failures. More anxiety compounds the mammoth guilt already being carried by parents.

THE NEW CODE: Autonomy

We need to reclaim our capabilities as parents.
We are a powerful force in the lives of our
children. We feel so inadequate and scared of
doing something wrong that we crumble under
the pressure, losing trust in our children and
ourselves.

We so fear our children and doing something wrong that we would
rather they were in the care of someone else, because we've come
to believe that this someone else knows how to do it better than
we do.

We do not need to check with psychologists, educationalists or the medical profession every step of the way. If the experts were right, we would have seen a massive positive societal change.

Down with Experts!

The majority of parents out there are good parents, trying to do their best in their own circumstances. We don't hear about them very often but they *are* there.

Many of these parents are buying into the idea that the answers to their children lie with an expert. Believing this, they buy the flashcards and intelligent toys. They sign up their kids for lesson after lesson and provide them with every resource they can. If this behaviour was what breeds genius, we'd see an abundance of Einsteins in every classroom across the country. But we don't. Instead, we hear of how many children cannot read or write, who are incapable of learning. We see children who have lost their imaginations and their capacity to let go and be a child, because to be a child is unacceptable.

If we look to those individuals who have become humanity's greats, we will often see that behind them was a parent or significant individual who *knew the child* and who was strong enough to encourage their child's individuality and talents. Many of these greats would have failed in our education system, labelled as stupid or dyslexic or ADHD. Their mentors didn't have a rulebook with a set of instructions for the making of a genius. They relied on the nature of the child and their own intuition and intelligence.

Down with Money-Hungry Executives!

We parents are worth a lot of money. We want the best for our children and are quite prepared to pay top dollar for it. The marketing executives know it and much of our buying power is geared towards making our child *more* – intelligent, musical, multilingual and creative. While you may have some holistic ideal about what you are providing your child, very often there is also some form of fiscal gain to be made by making you believe the information.

It is not only you that is worth big bucks, but also your two-year-old. And your seven-year-old. And then there's your 14-year-old. Child development research has not been used just for helping our children; advertising and marketing experts have studied it to learn how to attract children and teens to their product. Certain industries endeavour to make your child a lifelong customer from their toddler years.

As a parent you are battling with the images your child is being bombarded with on television, on the radio, at the supermarket and even as they walk down the road.

Take, for example, the supermarkets and shops that do not provide a child-friendly checkout for parents to use. Now, at child number four, I realise that it is a young child's nature to throw a fit when they cannot have the chocolate that is displayed at their height-level. If they cry or scream, I give them a cuddle and meet the eye of the disapproving checkout operator. I never, ever apologise. If the store owners are intent on manipulating parents like this, then I am not going to expect my two-year old to understand.

As they get older, you can help your child become more discerning, but the two-year-old screaming at you for a toy or chocolate bar literally cannot comprehend your well-reasoned denial of their needs. You may be filled with guilt and feeling like a failure for denying your child the right to have what they so desperately need, but you are in control, you know what is the best thing for them, and you are the one that needs to maintain control of their buying habits.

Becoming Discerning Parents

To make choices regarding purchases, we must first make choices regarding the information that we are given. We've got to become very selective about that which we hold as accurate and worthwhile. We can find parenting books by the dozens, parenting magazines, parenting websites, parenting courses and classes. It would be closed-minded to say that all information is bad or useless, just as it would be ignorant to assume that all the available information is worthwhile and valid.

Despite all the drawbacks of the information age, there are also a number of positives. Spock, for example, has not been around to witness the leaps in scientific understanding of human development. Most relevant to his work would be the discoveries made about how the brain grows in the years from birth to age three. To ignore such new information could be just as unwise as viewing all new information as equal.

We must be able to objectively view new information as it applies to us. This objective view will help us understand what the information actually means and whether or not we should act upon it.

That brings us to the next question: how on earth do we wade through the child rearing cornucopia and get to the real stuff – the meaningful stuff?

Code THREE

THE OLD CODE: Indulgence

In October 2004, CBS presented information about the Y generation, labelling them the 'Echo Boomers' – the children of the Baby Boomers.

They are the largest generation grouping since the 1960s, the first to grow up technologically connected. They are also worth a fortune in their spending habits. In the USA alone, the echo boomers are spending some US$170 billion per year. These children are, above all, *indulged* – emotionally and materialistically.

The CBS report gave voice to what most observant members of society had already noticed. The boomers had an 'ideal' upbringing and then fought against it – drugs, sex and *me* became important. And then they became parents. Wanting the absolute best for their children, they believe that indulgence is the name of the game. Forget the rebelliousness of their own youth, this group wants their children to have it all.

The indulgence mentality comes from a belief that as parents we are responsible for everything our children think, feel and do. It comes from a belief that we can protect our children from every harm and hurt in life. Having fought authority and restrictions, many of today's parents do not want to turn around and be the authority figures in their children's lives – it goes against their fundamental belief system.

Parents have also, for the first time in history, married because they wanted to (if at all), and had children when they chose. Families have shrunk in size, making each child all the more precious and in need of serious indulgence.

Types of Indulgence

There are two main ways of indulging children:

1. The first is *emotional*. This stems from the idea that we want the emotional bonding with our child that is often talked about in books and magazines. Parents today care very deeply about their child's emotional development – perhaps more so than in the past. This emotional bonding goes hand in hand with a desire to be our child's best friend. Best friends are equal partners, not one being the boss of the other. Some parents want the relationship with their children that they never had with their parents.

2. The second main indulgence is *materialistic*. Some parents want their children to have everything that they never had, while others want to give their children everything that they *did* have. While Baby Boomers are labelled as indulged emotionally, Generation Xers are labelled as being indulged materialistically – a generation with well-stamped passports, computers, televisions, videos, toys and so on. And maybe there is a piece of us, way down deep, that above all else wants to be *liked*. We want to be good parents, and one way of knowing we are a good parent is that our child likes us.

Consequences of Indulging Our Children

The intention behind indulging children is, I'm sure, very positive. I am also sure that most parents do not want to deal with the consequences of overindulged children.

Over-indulged children grow up believing that the world is an easy place, where their every desire will be met. They have an unrealistic perception of life – that they will come out of school as a CEO of a major company with car, mobile phone, computer and salary equal to their parents. Self-centred and spoilt, they can quickly become angry, unmotivated and envious.

Indulged children are also more likely to be lacking in self-control. Never having experienced delayed gratification, and choices with regards to sex, drugs and alcohol will be made 'in the moment' rather than looking at the longer-term consequences.

Recently, we've also seen that indulged children are prone to violence – against their own parents.

Hey, let's get really honest here – indulged children end up spoilt little brats. You know who they are – the whining, manipulative and greedy little beings that we see every time we go to a playground. We see them at birthday parties and in their own homes. They treat their parents like crap and they walk around with a chip on their shoulder.

Indulgence – whether it is materialistic or emotional – ultimately leaves our children on the back foot. Unaware of their own limitations, they see only their greatness and forget about things like being humble and showing empathy towards others.

Each child of mine has become easier when it comes to behaviour (although Madeline has to take the cake for stroppiness), so I'm forced to ask myself – is it their 'natural' temperament or is it me that has made the difference?

If I am completely honest with myself, I have to say that it has come from me. And Tony, of course. When Kalym was a babe and then a toddler, I was hooked into the belief that I was solely responsible for everything he experienced. I didn't want him to know pain or loss, so I was petrified of doing something wrong. His emotional well-being was of the utmost importance, and therefore his anger, tears or frustration were things that I felt I was experiencing myself. I'd feel guilty, and beat myself up for it.

Then came a day when he was four. I was putting Kalym into bed. He started whimpering.

'What's the matter?' I asked, filled with motherly concern.

'I'm scared,' says he.

'What of?'

'Monsters! They're in the closet!'

That my four-year-old should be suffering from such delusions was heartbreaking. With painstaking care, I opened the closet and showed him that there was no monster. Still not reassured, we talked through his fears, to no avail. After half an hour I asked him if he'd like Dad to come and talk to him.

'Yes, please,' he whispered, looking at me with his big blue eyes opened wide with concern.

I walked into the lounge where Tony was sitting playing at the keyboard. I told him that Kalym was in his bedroom scared of monsters and that I couldn't reassure him and asked him to go and try. Tony nodded and then kept playing. After a few minutes I started getting annoyed with him – did he not realise Kalym was suffering?

Another five minutes and Kalym comes out into the lounge, tears hinting at his eyes. Without looking up, Tony sent him back to bed. By now, I was outraged at Tony's apparent lack of caring.

Finally he walked to Kalym's room and came back some two minutes later. 'He's fine, now,' he said.

There was no way I could believe that – he had been so upset.

'He was having you on,' said Tony.

Now this was getting too much – my dear child manipulating me? Never!

As it turned out, he was. Tony had walked into Kalym's room and said: 'You're having your mum on, aren't you?'

Kalym had giggled, then nodded his head.

'You're not scared of monsters, are you?'

A shake of his head.

'Then lie down and go to sleep.'

'Okay.'

And that was it! I still kick myself to this day.

So, when Lachy did his four-year-old 'I'm scared of monsters' thing, I merely said to him that he had the magic powers to make them go away. I didn't make a big deal of it. And guess what? Neither did he.

THE NEW CODE: Temperance

This new code refers not to the total abstinence of alcohol, but to the ability to display self-control and restraint.

First we must give up the idea that we are in every way, shape and form responsible for every feeling and experience our child has. Guess what? We are not responsible and we are unable to afford that protection. In fact, it is an egocentric view. We are not so important that we can have a total effect on how another human being behaves and how successful they are in life.

We are told again and again how much impact we as parents have on the happiness and future success of our children. We take such huge responsibility for our children's behaviour that we are going to be behind before we've even begun.

There are some things our children do or are going to do that we do not understand and in no way modelled for them to copy. And their behaviour starts young. Take my youngest, Madeline. By nine months of age she was a biter. If someone took something she wanted or she didn't get her own way she would bite them. Hard. None of my other children bit her, I certainly didn't bite her and she wasn't exposed to other children who would bite her. *She just did it!* It was a self-defence mechanism that had nothing to do with how she was being raised.

Then there's Malachy. When we are out and about, he walks up to strangers and says, 'I don't like you.' Because he is child number three, I'm not very self-conscious about this, although I do apologise on his behalf. But, again, I didn't teach him to do this, and as far as I am aware he didn't observe other people doing this either.

Temper tantrums are another example. If a child is in a shop and starts a tantrum that causes people to stop and stare, stay calm. Your mission is to get you and your child out alive.

Children are going to be children. They are going to have their own interests, their own feelings, and their own life path. We can help them on the journey but there are a huge number of other factors that are going to shape their behaviour, not least of which is their genetic disposition. You cannot and will not be with your children 24 hours a day, seven days a week throughout eternity. Would you really want to be? You would ultimately be depriving your children of life experiences. The fact is, other people and other experiences are going to help shape your child.

This doesn't mean that if you neglect a child, or abuse a child, or refuse to cuddle and nurture a child that you are not responsible for later delinquency and problems. Of course a child raised in this environment will suffer. But on the flip side, it is unwise to blame yourself every time your child does something embarrassing, rude, dangerous or mean. Consider your own history – would you credit your parents with everything that you are today, both the positive and the negative? I doubt it. So don't hold yourself solely responsible for your child's behaviour either. We're important, but not that important.

The Power of No

We are allowed to say no and mean it. Your child will not suffer for the rest of their life if they do not get the latest toy that they so desperately need. The fad will pass in a month, and the next thing will come along. They may scream, shout and throw a tanty but if you say no – stick to your guns.

Children are super-quick learners and will learn that when you say it, you mean it, and they will lose all motivation for trying to emotionally manipulate you into getting what they want.

However, I am always careful to pick when to say no. Some parents seem very good at saying no when it is to prevent a child from doing something. I was once at a playground just after a rain patch and a mother marched in with her nicely dressed daughter. My boys were up on a roundabout having a ball and the little girl moved towards them. The only problem was that in order to get onto the roundabout, she had to step through mud. You can imagine her mother's alarm at getting those nice white shoes dirty! She was quickly dragged away to do something more 'appropriate'.

Not getting dirty seems to be a biggy. I see this quite often. I view getting dirty as a natural and *necessary* part of being a child. Mud and rain are of the utmost interest to young children – the sound of drops, catching water, finding worms, feeling mud (possibly even tasting it), is the child exploring their world.

Baths are designed to get children clean. Use them.

Discipline

No discussion of indulgence would be complete without talking about discipline.

There are many books available on this topic. Some identify the personality type of your child and then examine what type of discipline is going to work best for them. Some talk about 'time out', some use no discipline (we must talk through everything), and some have a set of instructions to follow in a 20-point system involving rewards and punishment. Yes, I exaggerate, but really, when did we get so obsessed about needing advice for disciplining our children?

So, without wanting to sound like a know-it-all, here's some things that I've learned on the parenting journey that seem to work for my family:

• **Respond immediately in whatever form of discipline you feel most appropriate.** There isn't an absolute way to discipline your child. You are the adult – act like it and move on. If they need a quick telling-off, do it. If they need to go to their room, do it. If they need to be ignored, do it. If they need to be punished, then just do it – quickly. Sometimes all you need to do is look at them and they know what you are thinking. You may respond to one thing differently because you are out and about. You may know that your child has had a bad day and respond differently on another given day.

• **Expect good behaviour.** Your child will live up or down to whatever expectation you have. If you think that your two-year-old shouldn't have to say please or thank you, then they won't. If you think that they should, then they will. If you think your four-year-old shouldn't have to help tidy up, then they wont. If you think that they should, then they will. If you expect your 14-year-old to contribute to the home, they will. If you expect them to enjoy their years and not have to shoulder any responsibility, they will do this too.

• **Like the child, dislike the behaviour.** This is one of the most important ideas for me. Sometimes children drive you wild with choices they've made or things they are doing. Our response – anger, disappointment or sadness – is natural. We are allowed to feel this way. And the child can know about it – but they don't need to be attacked *personally*. No name-calling. Simple as that. Direct whatever emotion you are feeling at the behaviour, not at the child. It leaves both you and your child with your dignity.

Code FOUR

THE OLD CODE: Time-Deficiency

This responsibility we feel for our children's happiness and future success means that we are often given the message that we are not spending enough time with our children.

This popular comment is generally directed at the working parent. It is backed up with oodles of research and is the number one guilt-causing thought pattern of today's parents. But let's examine this basic assumption for a moment. Most families require both parents to be working in order to make ends meet. There has been a massive turnaround from the idealised 1950s woman who stayed at home with her children and kept her husband's slippers warmed by the fire, ready for when he came home from work (and relied on 'mother's little helpers' – AKA Valium and Halcion and other benzodiazepines – to get through the day).

For many families, this isn't an option. And for those families where it is an option, there are a number of other factors involved.

Attachment Theory

Without getting too bogged down with theory, a brief examination of 'attachment theory' is useful here, as this is the foundation that pushes researchers to highlight the need for parents to spend more time with their children. If you read the newspaper or watch television, you will be aware of studies and experts who regularly pop up with another piece of evidence to support the theory that all children should be in childcare – or all women should stay at home and look after their children.

Attachment, in simple terms, refers to the child's relationship with an 'other'. This could be a mother, father, grandparent, caregiver, peer, sibling or even a favourite blanket or toy. The idea behind attachment theory is that when a child has a secure attachment to a caregiver, they are able to venture out into their environment with confidence. It is, in our terms, *love*.

This theory has fuelled the likes of Freud and Doctor Spock to proclaim that this secure base *must* be with the child's mother. In order to have a secure, happy child, the mother must spend all day, every day with her baby and meet all of its needs. This line of thinking is coming back into popularity with some women who term themselves *attached mamas* and wear the baby in a sling, sleep with them in their bed, breastfeed on demand and don't leave the baby to cry. It is deemed the most natural way of raising a baby – and one that I was very strong on, particularly with Malachy.

Like everything else, there are a number of theories about attachment, each dependent upon any given expert's academic focus. Freud had a psychoanalytic theory which said that infants form attachments because they can fulfil their need for oral stimulation. There is the learning theory, cognitive developmental theory and the ethological theory. The latter is an approach that emphasises the reciprocal development of attachment – that is, that both mother and baby are becoming attached.

The importance of attachment

We can't get around it – all research indicates the importance of quality attachments in the early years. Attachment affects a child's continuing development.

High-quality attachments give a child a great head start in life:

* ✳ more confidence to explore, solve problems and maintain interests
* ✳ enthusiasm, persistence, cooperation
* ✳ greater happiness
* ✳ attentiveness
* ✳ willingness to participate in class
* ✳ higher grades at school
* ✳ greater empathy towards others
* ✳ social competence and skills
* ✳ higher self-esteem
* ✳ ability to form meaningful relationships with peers
* ✳ trust in the world as a 'good place'
* ✳ greater self-respect
* ✳ greater self-confidence and self-concept.

Becoming attached

Attachment is not formed at the instant you find out you are pregnant, nor at the moment the newborn takes its first breath. It forms through a series of stages, proposed by Schaffer in 1996:

* ✳ **0–2 months:** the baby is relatively indiscriminate in its social activity – which is why it is so easy to pass Baby around at this age.
* ✳ **2–7 months:** the baby is learning to discriminate between people it knows and doesn't know.
* ✳ **7–24 months:** the baby is now developing specific attachments and goes out of its way to be with its primary caregivers. Around this age the baby may become distressed by strangers or by a caregiver leaving them.

* **24+ months:** the child, over the next three years, begins to learn that its caregivers also have needs and feelings, and the relationship is more about give and take.

Quality of attachment

Mary Ainsworth studied the nature and quality of attachments in the 1970s and since then numerous studies have been done that confirm her initial conclusions that there are four different types of attachment:

* **Secure attachment:** a child seeks physical contact and interaction with the parent after they have been separated. The parent can easily reassure the child who can then return to its play fairly quickly
* **Insecure-avoidant attachment:** a child ignores their parent when they return from an absence
* **Insecure-resistant attachment:** a child is overly needy when their parent returns after a separation and is not easily calmed. This child may show some hostility or anger
* **Insecure-disorganised attachment:** a child cries for their parent and then runs away when they come for them, or as they get older they try to 'parent the parent' – directing the interactions by showing extreme emotion or by behaving in embarrassing ways.

Reciprocal attachment

The question now is: how do these attachments form? One of the big things to remember is that attachment is a two-way street. When it comes to forming a relationship with your child, however, your parenting style will be the biggest indicator of the quality of the attachment.

An autonomous parent who is sensitive to the needs of their child will be most likely to have a secure attachment. A parent who is dismissive of their child is likely to have an insecure-avoidant attachment. A parent who is preoccupied with other things, such as finances, or who is depressed is most likely to have an insecure-resistant attachment.

The Childcare Debate

If you have or did have a child in daycare, it doesn't mean that they are insecure and that your relationship with your child is of a lesser quality than that of a stay-at-home mother. We need to move away from an 'either/or' mentality. There are many factors that contribute to the physical, emotional and intellectual development of children in their first few years of life. The biggest pressure in any discussion about childcare is on the mother. We cannot get around the fact that having a secure relationship with Mum is important. But so too is a quality relationship with Dad, with grandparents and with peers.

Much research places the emphasis on Mum being permanently with her child – and most often this advice comes from observing other cultures or other mammals. So, here's a piece of anthropological evidence that may shock you:

Mothers are exclusive caregivers in around three per cent of human societies.

And here's another one:

In as many as 40 per cent of human societies, mothers are not even the major caregiver.

While these sorts of blanket statistics shoud be approached with caution, it seems it is *normal* for a child to form multiple attachments – dads, grandparents, peers, siblings and other significant adults are important to the child. The critical factor appears to be the *quality* of the attachments rather than the *number* of attachments. However, the number of attachments needs to be consistent – the child needs to know the important people in his or her life, not be shoved from one stranger to the next.

Because early attachments are important, when we consider daycare options we must look at who can provide attachments. Relationships are more important in the early years than trying to push a child towards early independence or academic achievement. I know, for example, that my children care very much for the staff at their daycare. They greet them with a cuddle, but they are just as happy to wave goodbye (most of the time, anyway – sometimes they want to stay there longer!). This is why the personality and autonomy of individual staff is so important – a staff member who is dismissive and insensitive to a child's needs will not provide the child with a firm attachment. If a child is in this environment for the better part of their week, there will be negative consequences.

At this age, the caregivers must be prepared to give cuddles and nurture the children in their care. Unfortunately, the risk and fear of sexual abuse has meant many adults feel insecure about giving physical nurturing. When I was teaching five-year-olds, I had a parent come up and ask what I would do if her daughter was hurt. She was most relieved to learn that I would give her child a cuddle if needed.

At our local kindergarten, which Lachy attends, there is a male head teacher, Dave. I am very pleased when I see him rough and tumble with the kids but also give a crying child a hug.

Effects of childcare

There have been many studies into the effects of daycare on children. Of primary importance to parents is whether childcare will affect the quality of their own attachment with their child. Research shows that the quality of attachment is not affected by children spending time in daycare. The number of hours spent in daycare, however, *can* affect the relationship between parent and child. Other studies have suggested that when a mother works full-time before the child is one, an insecure attachment is more likely.

However, evidence does show that parental *style* is a key factor. Some children, whether or not they have a full-time mother or are in full-time daycare, will be insecure, and some will be secure. 'Good parenting' as described by Desforges (2003), includes: 'a secure and stable environment, intellectual stimulation, parent-child discussions, constructive social and educational values, and high aspirations relating to personal fulfilment and good citizenship'. There! We can do that, can't we?

Because attachment forms over time, the parent and child need opportunities to be together in order to enable this to happen. A mother who dislikes caring for her baby will have an insecure attachment whether or not that child goes into daycare. But the opportunity to form an attachment with a significant other – that is, a childcare worker – may actually serve to overcome the later emotional, intellectual and social problems associated with children and adults who are unable to form close attachments.

If we look at the development of attachment outlined earlier, it would make sense for a baby to be introduced to another primary caregiver *before* the age of seven months. Hopefully by this age the child recognises both Mum and Dad as people who will meet their needs and who are dependable. If a child is put into daycare at two days old, I imagine that it would be difficult for the mother and infant to form a firm attachment.

Many studies have confirmed the long-term positive effects of childcare. The problem with most of these studies, however, is that they have been done in conjunction with a university and so the childcare studied was of a very high quality. Recently, there has been research into lower-quality care which confirms that it is the *quality* of the care provided to the child that matters, rather than whether the child is in care or not.

We know that the experiences of early childhood are changing, as more and more families require two incomes in order to meet their basic financial needs. Perhaps knowing this can help ease the guilt that parents feel with regards to spending 'enough' time with their child. So, assuming that some form of childcare is a necessity for the average New Zealand family, it is important to ascertain what *quality* childcare is. How do we sift through the multitude of options out there to find where to send our children or who to choose for home-based care?

Grandparents as caregivers

If you have help in the form of grandparents, I'd use it. My own parents were brilliant when I was raising Kalym on my own. While I worked,

Kalym was well looked after. They took long walks along the beach, read countless stories and had the patience that I was lacking. Such relief of stress cannot be underestimated.

Nannies

Nannies are another option. A good nanny provides the secure attachment that is important for this age group. Nannies are also more flexible in their hours and can assist in picking up and dropping off children at their various activities. Such an option, however, relies upon adequate finances. Nannies are expensive. Not only does the parent have to pay for the nanny's wages, but also their food and any resources that the child needs throughout the day.

I personally favour good-quality childcare centres over nannies. I am too nervous about leaving my children in the care of an adult who is unable to take a break, who will have mood swings, and who may or may not have the same expectations of day-to-day life.

Childcare centres, on the other hand, have a number of people working at them, so that if one becomes stressed, another can take over. There is more of a community feel, as one person does not have sole responsibility for all children at all times. A good programme will include important things like physical activity, art, creativity, books and the encouragement of independence.

Cost of childcare

No talk of childcare options would be complete without a discussion of cost. Childcare is expensive, and the more children you have, the more money you'll be paying. For the average-income New Zealander, childcare fees can make up a substantial portion of any disposable income.

The working solo parent with just one child, earning an average income and paying off a student loan, will pay a large chunk of their salary towards childcare. This is often the woman. The male, on the other hand, can work and has only a portion of his salary taken for child support. So, in the case of a separated but working couple who earn the same income, the woman will be more financially responsible for the child than the man. Even if he pays $50 per week child support, this is added to her income and barely covers a half of a week of (subsidised) childcare. This does not include food, clothing, medical expenses and all the other associated costs of raising a child. The solo parent is unfairly pushed into financial near poverty unless either party has a substantial income.

Even for those families living on a dual income, childcare costs still influence choice. The Labour government, in the May 2004 Budget, changed the threshold for working parents, so that parents can now earn more than they could previously and still receive subsidies.

Even on a larger wage, childcare can take up a huge portion of a working family's salary. Sometimes flexible hours are required, so that in any family there may be childcare costs, nanny costs and babysitter costs.

The government has also promised 20 hours free childcare to all children aged three and four by 2007, but this applies only to community centres. Our local kindergarten is stretched so tight already that three-year-olds are not getting in until they are almost four. It is a good theory, and I will watch with interest to see how they implement this policy.

On February 1, 2005, Helen Clark stood in parliament to announce Labour's vision for our country. Included in this speech was the statement that Labour would be encouraging women into the workforce. By doing this, New Zealand's GDP per capita would rise by 5.1 per cent. Such a push was encouraged by the government putting more money into early childhood education, increasing childcare subsidies (something that has already benefited my family) and again, she promised 20 hours free childcare for three- and four-year-olds by 2007.

She then managed to stir the pot further by talking about increasing before and after school care for children aged five to 11.

Listening to her speech, I had a vision of her wearing Uncle Sam's hat, pointing a finger at the women of our nation with the cry, 'Women, Your Country Needs You!' In fact it annoyed me – more anti-family policy.

Instead of pressuring mothers, why not eliminate student debt so all those professionals working overseas can return to New Zealand?

Indeed, the proportion of so-called 'traditional' families, with Dad working while Mum stays home with the children, has decreased in New Zealand from 49.2 per cent in 1986 to 28 per cent in 2001. Surely this indicates that women (mothers) are already working harder?

Upon analysis, however, the opportunity for childcare and out-of-school care combined with the Working For Families package opens the doors for women to have *choice*. If a woman chooses paid work, she's supported, if she chooses unpaid work and a single income she is supported there also.

I have already mentioned the modern working parents' need for flexibility. Often the extreme view of such opportunities is that parents will dump their children in care for 12 hours a day and as such the children will suffer. In reality, however, I believe that given such opportunities, a woman (or man) may choose to work long hours for a time and then have a few days off – think of the ambulance and police officers who live this lifestyle. Or, parents may choose to work from early morning to early afternoon, knowing that their children will be cared for in good environments.

So, I think her theory is right; it was just presented poorly in a purely economic light that doesn't exactly scream *empathy* or *understanding*. The reality is, every parent is contributing to this country – in human capital.

Quality Childcare

How can we know what is a good childcare centre and what is not? My own experiences have been varied. In one centre, a teacher advised me to remove my child because the director of the place was hitting the children. I removed my child immediately and in a few short weeks the place was shut down.

In another centre, one of my children refused to go one morning because, he said, one of the teachers had hit him. I set up a meeting with the teacher and her supervisor, both of whom denied any such event. I

69

decided not to pursue the incident, but withdrew my children because my job was to put them first – which meant listening to what they were telling me.

At another Auckland centre, Kalym was well looked after and formed a very close bond with a particular teacher. This was encouraged and she remains in our hearts to this day. The centre where my children presently go, Honey Bear Cottage, has a consistent and loving staff. The under-twos teacher, Val, has looked after my three youngest children and all have adored her. The other staff are friendly and informative, and my children come home telling me how much they love them.

How on earth do we know what is good quality care when we look for a childcare centre? Mech (pronounced Meesh) White is the director of Honey Bear Cottage. I asked her to formulate a checklist for parents who are choosing a centre for their child. This is what she came up with.

Quality childcare has:

* high teacher/child ratios
* a stable staff
* quality equipment
* a clean, attractive environment
* a balanced programme.

To help you choose a childcare centre for your child, Mech created the checklist on the following page.

MECH'S GUIDE TO FINDING GOOD CHILDCARE

❏ Check the latest Education Review Office report – it's available on the Internet or at the centre.

❏ Visit the centre and rely on first impressions:

   ✳ How are you greeted?

   ✳ Does the place seem friendly?

   ✳ Do you feel lost and don't know where to go?

   ✳ Do the children seem happy?

   ✳ Do they play in small groups and individually?

   ✳ Is there room for children to run and be adventurous?

❏ Check teacher/child ratios:

   ✳ One teacher for every 3–4 children for children under 2 years.

   ✳ One teacher for every 7–8 children for children over 2 years.

❏ Ask about staff turnover – is it high?

❏ Ask about staff qualifications.

❏ Is there structure in daily routines for children to feel secure?

❏ Is there time and space for children to develop their own interests and friendships?

❏ Can children of different ages interact?

❏ What are the discipline procedures?

❏ How are parents kept informed about their child's progress?

❏ Are parents able to discuss their concerns and ideas?

❏ Find out the goals of the programme – does it have an academic or social focus?

❏ Watch staff and child interactions – are children respected and nurtured?

❏ Look at the environment:

   ✳ Are there accessible toilets and basins?

   ✳ Is it attractive and inviting?

THE NEW CODE: Time-Sufficiency

In between the theory and pressure of forming attachments, financial circumstances, temperament (of both parent and child) and the need for autonomy, we come to the new code – time-sufficiency.

We all want to give the best to our children, so often there is a pull to justify our choice of working or not working. In reality, however, we need to base our decisions on our own individual circumstances. Some children thrive in daycare, others are miserable. Some families can survive on one income or one and a half incomes, while others cannot.

If parent's pitch against each other it helps no one and only highlights feelings of guilt and inadequacy. It is not working-parent versus at-home parent. There are only options and choices.

There is no right or wrong answer for all families, and there is no right answer for one family at all times. Needs and wants change. The mother who chooses to work full-time may decide that she wants to spend more time with her children, and cut her hours back or quit work altogether. The father who wanted to stay at home with his children may find that it is nothing like he expected, and returns to paid employment.

Finding a solution can be very hard, as there are *always* going to be pluses and minuses with any choices we make. The answer usually lies not in black or white but various shades of grey.

The goal is to make an informed choice based on personal circumstances, and then embrace the positives and not be consumed by the negatives.

Option One: The Stay-at-home Parent

The negatives

Women of today are not raised to be good stay-at-home nurturers. We were given an education that stimulated our brains and made us search for a career that would be personally meaningful. Many of us went on to university where we could indulge in pseudo-intellectual conversations and pretend to understand society and believe that we held the answers as we drank too much alcohol and turned our noses up at materialism.

We are the generation that has been brought up with the phrase '*Women can do anything,*' which, in retrospect, may well have read, '*Women should do everything.*'

The feminist revolution, the burning of the bras and growing of underarm hair were all around. Some women dressed in 'power clothes' – suits with shoulder pads that screamed the message that they were a force to be reckoned with. We learned that the women who *had* been at home were secretly resentful of their husbands and were leaving them, when their children had grown, to pursue a university education and high-flying career. We witnessed the supposed growth of equality between men and women and were subject to the constant message that in order to make it in the world we had to have a career.

'Don't rely on men,' was the mantra. 'You don't need them. You can do it all yourself.' The doors opened by the female revolutionaries were exciting. Opportunities became available for women in areas that had been previously restricted. Women were given the right to have brains that were worthy of respect. And as we grew in this environment we began to think more of ourselves. We were sexy, savvy and intelligent.

What a great time it all was. How grateful I am to those women. But how damn near impossible it is to then adjust to a lifestyle at home with children.

Being at home (day-in-day-out) with children goes against our upbringing. Suddenly, we have someone who is dependent on us for everything. Our lives require a total readjustment of both values and priorities. We were raised to put ourselves first, to use our intellect and suddenly we cannot. The issues that this creates are real and raw.

The issues

Strain due to the single-income lifestyle:
* real difficulties meeting basic needs
* no financial back-up or savings for the future
* poorer health and sometimes poorer education due to associated costs.

Tendency towards martyrdom due to:
* taking the moral high ground against partner and women who work
* having a need to give oneself a sense of self-purpose
* a self-sacrificing attitude.

High risk of depression due to:
* mammoth change in lifestyle
* isolation
* negative treatment by society.

The positives

It is not all doom and gloom for the stay-at-home parent. But the positives are often inner rewards that are rarely seen from the outside looking in. I view my time at home with a sense of personal achievement, in survival if nothing else. I am more patient, kinder and much more able to discern between the important and the not-so-important. I've a much thicker skin now. I'm more self-reliant and self-trusting. I work harder when I get the chance, and my life perspective is fuller.

There is something to be said for confronting and overcoming your own negative thoughts. It would be easy to define the mass depression that can accompany time at home with children as post-natal depression, but the subject is far more complex. Living a busy, mind-based lifestyle makes subsequently staying at home with a child all the more difficult. If nothing else, I've learned to be comfortable in my own mind in a way that would have probably taken me years to achieve had I not stayed at home with my children and faced myself.

I've learned to treasure the small things, and value the magical moments with my children. Things just don't bother me as much as they used to.

For families who choose to have children later, this option is much more viable. Often, careers are well-established, making taking time off easier, and these families are likely to have more financial resources.

It's a very tough but very rewarding road to travel.

The rewards

Personal growth:

* ✽ greater opportunity for self-reflection
* ✽ clarification of goals and values
* ✽ opportunity to become more independent and self-reliant.

More relaxed lifestyle:

* ✽ at least one parent without work-related stress
* ✽ less life-bustle
* ✽ child's needs (such as illness) do not add stress.

Being there:

- ✳ seeing baby's firsts
- ✳ attending school events
- ✳ being child's greatest influence.

Option Two: Full-time Employment

The negatives

> One day, just before an important meeting, the nanny phoned to say that Wendy had told her teacher that she feels sad because she doesn't get to spend enough time with me. I felt as though I'd been kicked in the gut. Not only was my daughter missing me, but also I had to find out via the nanny, via her teacher. When I arrived home that night, we sat down and had a chat and she told me that yes, she had said this to her teacher. I tried my best to explain that I needed to work and through her tears she nodded while guilt consumed me. I did not stop working. I needed to work for me. What I did do was make sure I made better use of the time we did have together.
>
> *Natalie*

The issues

High levels of stress due to:

- ✳ mothers forced to return to work when children are very young
- ✳ combined stress of high achievement in work and as a parent
- ✳ the parent (often Mum) putting himself or herself last.

Worker vulnerability due to:

- ✳ high expectations of performance level regardless of what's happening at home, such as sleepless nights
- ✳ workplace bullying because of the pull between being a parent and worker
- ✳ having to leave early or have many days off due to a sick child.

Limited time with child:

* ✳ missing those baby firsts
* ✳ missing out on school trips, achievements and activities
* ✳ may be less aware of what is going on with child.

The positives

> *I've always been a high achiever – setting goals for myself and then working to make them a reality. I was so looking forward to becoming a mother and staying at home and looking after my child. But when she came along, I got so claustrophobic sitting there all day. My mind kept going a hundred miles an hour and I felt anxious most of the time. I couldn't stand it. I lasted three months, and then hired a nanny to look after her while I returned to the more exciting career world. I deal with hundreds of thousands of dollars a day and I make decisions that affect many members of our society. It makes me feel worthwhile and successful.*
>
> *Emma*

Full-time work gave me an escape from the personal stresses in my life. When I was at home all day, every day, problems seemed much larger and all-consuming. Work was a relief. Although it was often stressful, it gave me other things to think about and achieve, rather than focusing on what was happening personally. It was something that was all for me, that I was doing and had nothing to do with anyone else. Work was something I could hold on to, set goals for and whether I succeeded or failed, it was always challenging. I became more organised and a better worker. Because I would make the distinction between my role as mum and teacher, I knew that I was under time pressure to get things done at school so that it didn't interfere with my time with Kalym.

There are positives with maintaining full-time employment. The rewards can be huge both personally and professionally.

The rewards

More life opportunities due to:

* exposure to a variety of people
* exposure to a variety of experiences
* meeting career goals faster, and therefore being able to progress up the career ladder.

Less financial stress:

* more disposable income to provide for immediate needs
* more likelihood of having the opportunity to save for education and retirement
* greater choices in life.

Personal achievement due to:

* tangible goals and successes
* work achievements
* measurable societal contribution.

Option Three: The Part-time or Temping Parent

The scope of options available in the part-time or temporary employment category is huge and can include anything from the growing industry of home-based businesses, to working three hours a week at the local bookstore. 'Part-time' is an extremely loose term used to define a job that earns money on a less than full-time basis. There is a huge discrepancy between the number of hours worked and the levels of stress involved.

Temping is an option that may involve six weeks of full-time work, followed by six weeks off, or it could mean evening typing work of six hours per week.

Another possible option is job sharing, where two people share the workload of a single job and get paid accordingly. This requires working closely with the other person, where the needs of each are known and best attempts are made by each party to meet them. In an ideal situation, both parties are equal in capabilities and work ethic and get along fabulously. It has the potential to turn into a bitter relationship if one is constantly pulling up the other for not doing their fair share.

Another option is to establish and run a business from home. This is becoming an increasingly popular option with men and women alike, who are choosing to bow out of work outside the home to set up their own business. This can be a viable option but involves a degree of risk and requires previous experience. It can also be an isolating experience.

The negatives

The happy, idealistic balance that the part-time or temporary work option is said to offer can be somewhat of a farce. My experience as a part-time worker has at times been frustrating and I've often found that instead of achieving balance, I've gained the stresses of work combined with the depression of stay-at-home mothering. I have found it harder to define myself with part-time work because I'm neither a stay-at-home parent, nor can I commit to a career. Because most of my work has been home-based, I have still lacked the much-needed adult contact time.

On low weeks I feel incapable of juggling the complexities of each of the worlds I work in. The business takes its toll on me mentally. I resent not having the extra time for all the chores that need to be done around the house, let alone the 'me' time that we all need. My laundry spews dirty washing at me and I wonder if a) I should become a full-time mum and have more time for playcentre, mums' networking groups, housework, etc. or b) work full-time and support my partner more in the business, and leave my childcare to someone else.

I am stuck between two worlds, and like any decision we make in regard to looking after little ones it has its pluses and its minuses and its PRESSURES. I try to remind myself it is such a short time – I have one child at school already and she was just a baby yesterday. I don't want to wish their lives away, but sometimes it's tough. My only hope is I raise strong and happy children, and through this process also become a stronger person myself.

Geena

The issues

Frustration and feelings of inadequacy due to:

* the combination of stresses that the stay-at-home parent and the working parent face
* finding it harder to move up the career ladder – not working at full potential
* not fitting into category of either worker or stay-at-home parent.

Superhero Syndrome due to:

* combination of two full-time roles
* tendency to be all things to all people
* inability to justify time off – work is time off from the kids, and vice versa.

Harder to make any real impact on levels of disposable income due to:

* no or few associated benefits of full-time employment, such as sick pay and holiday pay
* less opportunities for promotion and employee vulnerability – hours can be cut easily without much notice
* generally lower pay if in part-time work.

The positives

On a good day, part-time or temporary work provides a balance between the stress of full-time work and the pressure of full-time motherhood. It makes it easier to have a sense of self-esteem and it does bring in extra income to the home, easing the financial strain of relying on one income.

> *I have good (energy) weeks and bad (exhausted) weeks. On good weeks I feel like my world is in balance. I bounce out of the house happy to escape my own four walls and be in a world with adult interactions, new mental stimulations and free from the chaos of early childhood. I am sure that working part-time has enabled me to keep my confidence levels elevated. On completion of my weekly hours I am happy to return to my loving children (who have usually been having a grand time with Granny or Nana) and be Mum extraordinaire once more.*
>
> *Geena*

The rewards

Life balance:
* opportunity to be there for the kids
* ability to keep mentally stimulated
* a compromise between the two extremes.

More opportunity for control:
* more flexibility in working hours
* ability to choose the amount of work taken on
* technology means there is more scope for suitable workspace and meeting deadlines.

Keeping employment opportunities open:
* maintaining worker connection – many employment opportunities come from 'who you know'
* harder to return to workforce after years away
* maintaining skills in a particular field.

Maintaining perspective

As we are constantly bombarded with the claim that we are not spending enough time with our children, it is refreshing to remember that staying at home has its negative consequences too.

A parent can spend all day every day with their child and never really have a decent conversation with them. A parent can work 17 hours a day and never have a decent conversation with their child.

It is a matter of perspective and balance. You are not going to ruin your child, whatever choice you make. Time spent with children in their world is a luxury to the working parent and to the stay-at-home parent. Each has a busy life with a different focus, and each family has to make choices based on their own individual circumstances and not be fooled by an ideal that is inaccurate and unobtainable. I'm sure that some parents thrive at home, just as I am sure that some parents thrive in the workforce. Personally, I thrive when I have a balance between the two.

Code FIVE

THE OLD CODE: Peter Pan Syndrome

Hot on the heels of indulgence and guilt comes the ideal of the eternal youth. Peter Pan appears to be alive and well these days.

We seem to be indulging our children so much because of the immense pressure for us to make sure they are *happy*. We are being fed the belief (as with the perfectionism ideal) that it is our children's fundamental right to be happy. There is nothing wrong with this if we look at happiness in a broad context, but many of us confuse happiness with instant gratification and end up overindulging our wee poppet. Instead of having them take responsibility for age-appropriate activities, many of us run around doing everything for our child.

Ideals such as responsibility, self-control and contribution have taken a back seat to happiness. It is almost as if we fear that if we expect our children to live up to such ideals, we are depriving them of their emotional well-being. In other words, we are denying them happiness.

Ever feel guilty for asking your child to clean up the lounge or make their bed? Of course you have, because they put on the petulant look that says you are punishing them – confirming for you that if you expect them to do something you are depriving them of a precious moment of childhood by forcing them to grow up too soon.

Adolescence – the time of self-exploration – appears to be a stage that children are entering earlier and earlier and staying in longer and longer. There are many reasons for this – including the increases in living and education costs. Childhood toys, instead of passing by the wayside, merely change their face and financial value.

Personally, I find it all rather pathetic. Rather than raising our children to contribute to society, to be empathetic, to live up to their potential, the Peter Pan Syndrome encourages our children to stay as young as they can for as long as possible. Instead of learning self-reliance and responsibility, they learn frivolousness and selfishness.

I recently had a conversation with a 17-year-old boy, Tim, who I would consider mature for his age. In his last year at school, we had a chat about adolescence versus adulthood: What factors define these categories? What ensued was two hours of confusion. Neither of us could give a definitive answer. We both knew people in their late teens who were more mature in their thinking and actions than some other people in their 30s or 40s.

At first, when asked, he considered himself to be an adult because, 'I can make my own decisions and don't need to be told what to do. I also work and buy my own things.'

Delving further, he admitted that some of the teachers at his school still treated him as though he was a child and he found this frustrating and insulting. Shopkeepers never took their eyes off him. He couldn't legally buy alcohol until his 18th birthday, was still on his restricted licence and was unable to vote, but 'most teens don't care about that anyway'.

Tim then changed his mind, saying that the party to be held for his

18th birthday would be his public transition from adolescence to adulthood. It would, he said, be just like any other party, except bigger. His parents would be there in the background as well as any other family members he regarded as friends. Parents of friends would also come. There would be the usual drinking that accompanies the other teen parties he attends.

When asked what would be left to do at 18 that he had not already done, he thought for a moment and said, 'My 21st.'

When asked about things such as working and taking full financial responsibility for himself, or starting a family of his own, he said he considered these things secondary to the rites he had already passed through in his school years.

By the end of the conversation, we were both talking in circles. Despite this, his thinking was far more mature than many adults I know. He considered a major problem of the world to be overpopulation, believed that life should be simplified and that everything needed to slow down for a few years to give people time to reflect. The world as it is, is not a place he would want to raise children in; it was going to implode if it continued as it is.

On the flip side, he was restricted by financial dependence on his parents (something that will continue for many years because he is going to university), by the way some adults treat him ('they think they should get respect just because they're older'), and by the law.

The same conflicts confronted us when we tried to define when childhood ended and adolescence began.

Life's Turning Points

We lack, for various reasons, an ability to understand various phases of our life because there are few definitive turning points. These turning points were first called 'rites of passage' by anthropologist Arnold van Gennep, around 100 years ago. In his research, van Gennep found that throughout the world, people consciously marked turning points in their life cycle. These turning points are emotionally significant moments, such as birth, death, menarche and so on. Since van Gennep formulated his theories, there have been many scholarly explorations into the multilayered meanings behind these rites of passage.

To the Western thinker, the concept of a rite of passage connotes images of small-scale cultures and morbidity – mutilations, piercings, tattooings, circumcisions – taking place against a background of costume wearing, chanting and dancing community members. Religious rites also come to mind, such as those of the Catholic Church: baptism, first communion and confirmation.

The idea that these passages are for other people in other places is a limited view. Rites of passage occur in our society, whether we want to acknowledge them or not.

Return to the adolescent who gets his driver's licence, has sex for the first time or tries drugs or alcohol. These are modern-day rites – just watch any teen movie since James Dean popularised the journey through adolescence in *Rebel without a Cause*. Lacking societal and parental influence, adolescents have created their own rites of passage.

Let's also be clear: there are a number of adults (parents included) who subscribe to the Peter Pan Syndrome. Maybe it's time for them to grow up . . .

THE NEW CODE: Altruism

If, as I believe, the goal for both our children and ourselves is to become altruistic adults, we need to first look at what altruism actually means. Then we can look at some ways of achieving it.

From a theoretical perspective, the *humanistic psychologists* provide a sound view. They believe, unlike traditional theorists, that we are not passive recipients of past events and present circumstances. They believe that we are in a constant state of *creating* our personality and lives, using deliberation and insight.

Abraham Maslow

One of the prominent humanistic psychologists is Abraham Maslow, who put forward a concept known as the *'hierarchy of needs'*. In simple terms, this refers to an order of needs that must be met in order for a person to develop to their full potential.

According to Maslow, there are three levels of needs:

Fundamental needs

These include basic survival needs such as food, shelter, sex and safety.

Psychological needs

These are centred on emotion: love, the need to belong, self-esteem, to have approval, acceptance and acknowledgement.

Self-actualisation needs

These involve the need to fulfill one's own unique potential.

Down with Peter Pan!

Self-actualisation, according to Maslow, is not some selfish ideal where the *me* is the most important thing. Stepping on other people to get ahead is not being self-actualised. Not taking responsibility for choices and actions is not being self-actualised.

BECOMING SELF-ACTUALISED

In 1970, Maslow composed a list of characteristics of a self-actualised individual, which includes:

* a firm perception of reality
* accepting of themselves, other people and the world around them
* spontaneous
* problem-centred rather than self-centred
* private

* autonomous
* independent
* resists stereotypes, yet not deliberately flamboyantly unconventional
* sympathetic to the condition of others
* promotes welfare for all
* has deep, meaningful relationships with a few people as opposed to superficial bonds with many
* democratic
* creative.

Moving towards Altruism

In trying to construct our lifestyle (being the creative and active humans we are) we can consider the following points:

Fundamental needs

These are the most important needs to be met. Without food and shelter and without safety we will become stuck in a fight, flight or freeze pattern. Food gives us health and energy. If we are struggling to put food on the table, then it is very difficult to be thinking about bigger issues.

First, a family will need to ensure that there is adequate income coming in to cover housing and food costs. If this cannot be done on a single income, then both parents will need to work. Simple as that. No need for guilt strings to be pulled.

Second, an environment of safety is required. This includes emotional security.

Psychological needs

Once we have our basic needs met, we can then think about our psychological needs. Initially, the focus appears to be very much on our ability to have relationships – to feel as though we belong. We (and our children and partner) need:

✻ to belong to the family group – this means 'fitting in' to the family, not that we all must be the same, but that as individuals we can come together with respect and love. Family is a broad-ranging label that will mean different things within different families and cultures

✻ to have meaningful friendships – we are *not* all alone, holding up our portion of the world

✻ to be accepted for who we are.

The next level of psychological needs involves our feelings about ourselves:

✻ the need to achieve

✻ the need to be competent

✻ the need for approval and recognition.

Self-actualisation needs

Once there is enough income to meet needs, we have a supportive family and a good group of friends, we must then take a long, hard look at ourselves and try and decide what our *unique potential* is.

We will talk more about this unique potential later in the book.

Rites of Passage

In order to help our children and young people move towards altruism, we can bring back rites of passage – in a modern context, of course. These enable people to move through one stage of life to the other, while meeting the psychological needs that are so important.

Celebrating rites of passage provides an individual with opportunity for knowledge – both socially and personally.

Rites of passage celebrate who we are, while allowing us to be optimistic about what we may become. Returning to the adolescents: without adult contact and nurturing through the change into adulthood, they will rely on their peers to see them through. Peers *cannot* provide an understanding and appreciation of adulthood because they have not been there. This is something that only someone who has 'been there, done that' can do. However, to rely solely on parents to be the initiators into adulthood is also limiting. These are just two people (or three, or four in step-families) who can only give their own perspective. There needs to be other adults available for support – grandparents, parents of friends, friends of the family, aunts, uncles and so on. Life's transitions can create turmoil hormonally, emotionally, intellectually, sexually and spiritually.

If we choose to ignore these transitional phases, we are helping to create feelings of confusion, self-doubt and to encourage the effects of these feelings, such as violent acts against others or oneself.

Public acknowledgement of rites of passage provides safety and assurance to the individual.

Rites of passage mean individuals are not alone. They have other people who support them. The paradoxical nature of our society means that we hold individuality as near sacred and yet are also still dependent upon societal acceptance.

Rites of passage move each individual towards adulthood.

The ability of humans to become functioning, thriving adults has been explored by scholars at length. 'Self-actualisation', as it is termed by Maslow, or 'individuation' as it is termed by Carl Jung, requires not only self-knowledge but also an understanding of others.

Adulthood can only be described subjectively. It is becoming increasingly popular for people in their 20s, or even their 30s and 40s, to remain in adolescence: egotistical, materialistic, addicted, immature, selfish, too idealistic and lacking in responsibility both for themselves and for society.

By celebrating rites of passage, we encourage children to move into adolescence and support them through their natural rebellion. We encourage teens to move into adulthood and experience the trials and tribulations that they will be faced with.

THE RITES-OF-PASSAGE CYCLE

Van Gennep outlined three stages that a person goes through in moving from one cycle to the next.

1. **Separation:** saying goodbye to the cycle just ending, usually with a symbolic act of shedding the past.
2. **Marginal or liminal:** a time of transition where the individual is no longer categorised as they were before but they are not yet ready to move on to their new role.
3. **Aggregation:** entry into the next cycle of life.

These three phases were universal, regardless of culture. At the same time, the celebrations were socially and culturally specific.

Modern Rites of Passage

It would not be wise to celebrate these passages in ways that do not suit our culture. Sending a boy off into a forest for a week when his voice breaks to learn survival techniques, or shaving your daughter's hair and eyebrows when she gets her first period will probably do very little for your child and would very likely see CYFS knocking on your door. And unless you have highly self-confident and dramatic friends and family, dancing around a bonfire with masks on will not work either.

What follows are my attempts at generating ideas for celebrating rites of passage within *our existing society*.

There is no point in pretending to be that which you are not.

Birth

The celebration of a birth is often more for the parents than the newborn. The rite of passage, the change from being a foetus to a baby, occurred in the journey down the birth canal. Any celebration is of a welcoming sort, the entry into the human world.

The celebration of a birth is twofold, particularly if this is the parents' first child. Upon finding the woman pregnant, the couple begins the separation phase and moves into the marginal world of pregnancy – neither parent nor 'non parent'. When their baby is born the couple join the new world of parenthood. At such a celebration, everyone acknowledges both the child and the new role of the parents.

Naming ceremonies, baptisms, christenings or just gatherings of friends and family are symbolic acts of this new phase of life. Gifts are often brought for both baby and mother.

From infancy to childhood

While the first birthday may be seen as a passage from infant to toddler, it is difficult to pinpoint exact moments or celebrate in a way that is meaningful to the child.

By a child's seventh birthday, however, they have firmly moved through the early childhood phase. The transition period begins around the third year of a child's life.

At **four**, if self-care skills have been developed, the child has acquired some independence. They will also have experience in kindergarten or preschool.

At **five**, they have started school, another leap in independence. The earliest years at school begin the journey into learning the written language and adapting to new expectations and routines.

By the **seventh** birthday, most children will be able to read and write, are accepted into their new social status and place more importance on their peer relationships. They will also have begun the physical change of losing baby teeth.

Stage One: Separation – the fourth birthday

* In the few days before the birthday, gather together all the child's 'baby toys' in a box or a bag. Talk about how he or she doesn't need baby things anymore. On the day of the birthday give the toys away – either to a younger brother or sister, a local charity, or to an adult known to the child who is pregnant or who has recently had a baby. This is a symbolic act of moving away from babyhood.

- Celebrate the birthday with a party, inviting friends and family.
- Talk about the new expectations for the child – at this age the child can have their own jobs to complete around the home.

Stage Two: Transition – the fifth birthday

Starting school:

- visit the school several times before the first day. Get to know the teacher and the environment
- buy a new school bag and stationery supplies about a week in advance
- pack your child's schoolbag the night before
- if both parents are working, arrange for one of you to have the morning off work to accompany the child to school
- don't expect adjustment to occur immediately. The child may be grumpy and tired after school or go through a 'honeymoon' phase and come crashing down two or three weeks later. Emotionally support your child through this.

Developing friendships:

- invite new friends to come and play – get to know them
- gradually increase the amount of time the child is allowed to spend at a friend's house. Get to know their parents too
- keep lines of communication open. There will very likely be some form of conflict with peers or teachers and it is the parent's job to help the child cope with this.

Learning and home responsibilities:

- help your child set up a routine for doing homework
- help them with new skills needed for self-care or looking after the home.

Stage Three: Entry into childhood – the seventh birthday

- Give your child a present: a scrapbook of photographs and notes about their early years. This might be a book of 'My Firsts' or 'My Achievements', such as first word, step, day at school, friend, clothes, house, holiday, train ride and so on.

* Invite family to look through photographs and videos of early childhood.
* Celebrate the child's birthday with family and friends in a special place, such as the zoo or at an adventure park.
* Spend time with your child, redecorating their bedroom, removing baby accessories and colours.

From childhood to adolescence

Stage One: Separation – the 10th birthday

* Have your 10-year-old go away with their parent of the same sex. Spend two or three nights together and have a special birthday dinner at a restaurant (not fast food!). In the long hours together, share stories of childhood and talk about the changes that are already happening to their body or will soon be coming – the 'puberty talk'. Let it come from you rather than peers, as even in this 'advanced' society, some serious misinformation still persists. Don't just discuss the physical changes – remember emotional and hormonal ones too.

Stage Two: Transition – the 11th or 12th birthday (generally)

Onset of menarche or voice breaking:
* have a mother-and-daughter or father-and-son afternoon. If either parent is not available, use significant other
* treat your daughter or son to a visit to the beauty therapist's for a facial
* buy a special facial wash – skin care becomes very important
* talk about how important cleanliness is: daily showers and so on
* talk about what happens to the opposite sex
* discuss the significance of menstruation or voice breaking. They may be far from sexually active or may already be active but they need to know that they now carry the responsibility of the ability to conceive
* talk about sex. Contraception needs to be discussed, as do the emotions associated with sex. Again, do not leave this to other people, particularly peers
* this talk is not a lecture, but a discussion that allows their feelings to be acknowledged as well as a sharing of the parent's personal history.

Increase in personal responsibilities:

* personal cleanliness is now their responsibility; school is becoming increasingly their responsibility. Encourage commitment to a sporting or artistic activity.

Increase in household responsibilities:

* have the child assist in more activities such as washing, cooking and gardening
* support the child in moving schools – either intermediate or secondary.

Stage Three: Entry into adolescence – the 13th birthday

* Arrange a holiday between the new adolescent, the same-sex parent, plus any other friends or family of the same sex.
* Have the teen experience a 'thrill' such as a bungy jump or black-water rafting.
* Spend the night alone outside in a tent.
* Give the teen a piece of jewellery such as a pendant or ring to celebrate their change.
* This is another opportunity for redecorating their bedroom in a more appropriate style.

From adolescence to adulthood

Stage One: Separation – the 18th birthday

* Have a party with champagne – symbolic of their reaching the legal drinking age.
* Discuss new responsibilities. They need to take on a part-time job and contribute financially to the home. They are now just as important in making family decisions, and will be involved in them.
* In order to encourage a wider life perspective, give your young adult 10 books that you consider to be important in developing this. Preferably they should include stories and attitudes that are different from the 18-year-old's present circumstances, that is, different in place and thought. Tell them that they can choose a place in the world to travel to and you will match dollar for dollar their savings as a 21st birthday gift.

Stage Two: Transition – the 19th or 20th birthday

* Beginning tertiary studies. They are now responsible for their education. If you can afford it, pay for their education to avoid student-loan debt but only on the proviso that they pass their courses each year.

* If they choose not to further their education, but to work instead, they take on full adult rights *and* responsibilities within the home.

* Some may move out of the family home. There is plenty to learn in the flatting experience.

* The acquisition of assets, such as a car. This is their responsibility, so stay out of it – unless you want to purchase it for them, or at least assist in the purchase.

Stage Three: Entry into adulthood – the 21st birthday

* Have a birthday party, bringing friends and family together. Present photographs of the journey through childhood, have speeches and present the '21st key' of adulthood.

* As a present, give tickets to an overseas country and a backpack.

* Celebrate the adult that they are – their life purpose, their career path, and their ability to see through times of crisis, their relationships, their achievements and successes. Acknowledge all facets that make them whole, encouraging them to have a holistic view of themselves rather than as an egocentric and money-driven individual.

Code SIX

THE OLD CODE: Sophistication

You may be thinking, how can I claim in one breath that we don't want our children to grow up and in the next breath that we are pressuring our kids to be too sophisticated too early?

Fair question. But the two are not mutually exclusive. Both tendencies encourage today's children to reach adolescence at an early age, and to stay there as long as possible. There is a sophistication in today's children that appears obvious on the surface – children wearing teen clothing, having technological savvy and understanding the way the adult world works at a young age – and yet digging beneath this outer shell of sophistication generally reveals a child.

Every generation carries a different understanding of the world. My generation – the X Generation – carries, perhaps for the first time, a distinct lack of trust in the older generation. We were the first generation who grew up with television (and all its consequences), we were witness to the fallibility of adults and we were given a sophisticated view of life at an age when we didn't need it.

Today's children are encouraged to be sophisticated even earlier. They *appear* to be much more self-confident, savvy and intelligent. Just walk into any preschool or school in the country and you can see it. Talk to any teacher and you will hear about it.

But there are many problems associated with pushing our children to grow up too fast – to be sophisticated beyond their years. These children are missing out on their fundamental right to play, to create, to explore in a secure and safe environment. They have cellphones and Eftpos cards but don't know how to spend a couple of hours in the back garden without toys.

The focus appears to be on getting our children as worldly as possible, as early as possible – and we seem to forget that they are not little adults. They need time to mature emotionally, physically and intellectually. While research proves again and again the capacities of the brain for accelerated learning, we need to remember that beneath it all there is a child whose emotional maturity is of utmost importance. Return to Maslow's hierarchy of needs – if we raise a generation of insecure and emotionally immature children, what we can expect when they become adults is a nation of adults that look only to satisfy their own needs at the expense of anyone else; a nation of adults that want more and more toys and who find it difficult to maintain relationships. We see it today, don't we?

There has been some backlash to this mentality. More parents are choosing and monitoring what their child views on television and what games they play. More parents are stepping out of the 'rat race' so that their children are not subjected to it.

In many circumstances, this is not possible, regardless of intentions.

The most important thing to do initially is to really *look* at how we want the world to be. Then we need to look at the type of adults we want in control of this world. We need to walk backwards, step by step, and look at why we find it necessary to have our children become sophisticated from a very young age. Is it going to make them happier? Is it going to make them want to contribute positively to the world? Is it about them, or us? Too often it's the latter.

Early sophistication – being sexually aware (and often active), being aware of the adult world far before they are emotionally able to deal with it – is only to their detriment. And, in the long run, to ours also. We are giving our children the intellectual and technological tools to behave like adults, without ensuring that they have a solid foundation of emotional maturity, ethics and wisdom.

Let's turn the tables on the pressure to raise sophisticated children, let's put it in the 'obsolete bin' and simplify things so that they have a chance to be children and to grow up secure and unselfish.

THE NEW CODE: Simplicity

The new code of simplicity requires that we understand what is happening in our children's world – what their needs are. This understanding will provide us with solid information in trying to ascertain what we can do for our children for both their short-term and long-term good.

Age 0-1

What's happening?

Your baby is born with all the brain cells he or she will ever need – around 100 billion. However, most of these cells are not connected, and in order for the brain to function effectively, these cells will need to form neuron connections – 85 per cent of which are completed by the age of three. These growing connections can be observed through normal milestones such as crawling, grasping and talking.

In the first year of life, these connections are forming at an incredibly fast pace in millions of different ways. Sensory experiences – touch, taste, sight, hearing and smell – are absorbed in the brain. This means that parents and caregivers have a massive impact on the neural connections that are being formed and then reinforced. How the brain develops is directly influenced by the environment and experiences that the child has – whether these are positive or negative. Yes, genes are important as they provide *potential*. The connections must be formed in the early years in order for the brain to grow towards its underlying genetic potential.

If a child misses out on these experiences through child neglect, it has massive implications. The result is, quite literally, a smaller brain.

Baby is learning trust versus mistrust – is the world a good or bad place?

Baby is learning whether it is safe to relax, knowing that he or she will be cared for, or whether the world is an unreliable place where their needs are not met. The second scenario, which can be due to parental fighting, violence and aggression, the child's crying and screaming not being responded to, all results in the baby being on edge. Continued exposure to stress results in the child feeling tense when reacting to new situations.

The baby must be able to form attachments and bond in meaningful relationships.

These relationships help provide the foundation for later maturation and experiences in life. They provide the foundation for social skills, being able to make decisions and solve problems.

Intellectual development

Intellectual growth cannot be differentiated from physical and emotional growth. As discussed above, brain connections are being formed *as a result of* physical and emotional development.

The parent's role

The role of the parent in this first year is simple: love the baby. Love encompasses nurturing, feeding, hugging, singing, rocking and talking. These things all help the child to grow – physically, intellectually and emotionally.

By simply meeting the baby's needs and responding to its cues, the parent is helping it to develop.

We obtain our advice from books and experts – and most advice is offered for raising children aged 0–1. Keep them in their cot for sleep, feed only every four hours, carry Baby at all times, feed on demand and create a family bed, bottle feed, breastfeed, go onto solid food early, don't go onto solid food, immunise, don't immunise . . . it's too much.

I suggest ignoring all the advice and believing what your gut tells you. Feed on demand or try to make some sort of routine. Sleep with Baby in your bed (this may be the only way for you to get some sleep) or put them in a cot (this also may be the only way for you to get some sleep). Breastfeed if you can; if you can't, don't beat yourself up or be consumed with guilt – move on to bottles and formula. If you want to be there for your baby 24 hours a day, seven days a week, great. Go for it and enjoy. If you don't find that works for you, get someone to help you or send Baby to a childcare centre for the hours that are comfortable for you.

My four children were each raised differently in their first year. As a solo mum with Kalym, I needed sleep, so he slept in a cot and I taught him to sleep through the night by leaving him to cry for progressively longer intervals. He was weaned at six months.

Lachy was premature and seemed in constant pain for the first months, so Tony and I spent hours walking him up and down the hallway. He didn't have the strength for the sucking reflex and I couldn't stand the cow-like feeling of expressing, so he went on to the bottle at six weeks.

Malachy, who was born just one year and five days after Lachy, ended up in my bed to sleep. I couldn't get up and down to him all night and it was easier for me. He was weaned at 17 months.

Madeline started off in my bed, then moved to a cot at around a year.

I was getting depressed and stressed so I taught her to sleep just as I did Kalym. The idea of 'sleeping when Baby sleeps during the day' to catch up on sleep was not an option with two other preschoolers in the house.

So my advice is this:

Trust your instincts, do what's best for you and your children and ignore the dogmatic views of others.

All a baby needs is love, attention, a range of experiences and its basic needs met. Get a good support network, even if it means paying for it, and try to enjoy it. Stimulate your baby's senses – go for walks, sing to them as much as you can, set up your home so it is safe to explore.

Don't get hung up on developmental milestones – your child will learn to talk and to walk but will do it in their own time, at their own pace. Let them evolve as they are ready and do what you can, as you are able.

Don't buy into the subversive competitiveness of parents (particularly mothers) who skite that their child is sleeping through the night or feeding at those perfect four-hourly times. Who cares? Forget what other people's babies are doing – your only focus is your own child. It doesn't matter if your child walks at seven months or at 20 months. In fact, I have seen some research that indicates that babies who walk early do themselves no intellectual favours, as extended crawling helps in developing connections across the left and right brain hemispheres in a way that walking does not. I've also read that early walkers do not have firm attachments to their caregivers and that learning to walk early is an effort to get away from their mother.

I've also come across research of Marcelle Geber who spent time with 300 Ugandan babies – all of whom were crawling by six weeks and running at six months, so strong was their bond to their mother. The theory behind this is that these mothers, through natural birthing processes and holding their children at all times, meet their childs' needs. The babies, for example, do not wear nappies and yet never soil themselves. Why? Because these women have the ability to 'sense' when their child needs to toilet, and takes them into the bush where they can do so. I take my hat off to them!

Based on their firm attachment, the children have low levels of stress. In our Western culture, practices such as isolating children during sleep, keeping everything quiet, putting children into their cot to 'cry it out' contributes to their stress. As such the babies focus on basic survival needs. These Ugandan babes do not suffer the same stress and can therefore concentrate on learning about themselves. As such, they smile within an hour of birth, they crawl early and they walk early. Their intellectual development was considerably superior to their Western world counterparts until around the age of four. Feeling the old guilt strings being pulled? Don't, because interestingly enough, these 'super-mums' are culturally programmed to dump their children at this age — they literally become invisible to their mothers and are sent away to a different community to be raised.

So what is the answer for parents in the Western world? Just try to go through your day with Baby alongside you. Stop when she needs you, and involve her when you can. Dance with her; play with her and, most important, laugh with her. But also look after yourself.

This first year is for your child to develop secure relationships. Some will tell you this must be Mum; others will tell you that multiple attachments are best. Be honest to yourself about who you are and the feelings that you have, and make decisions based on that.

Ages 1-4

What's happening?

These are exciting years for both parent and child, as it seems that the child is learning something new every day! Each day, they become more and more independent physically, emotionally and intellectually. The massive changes that occur in these years are more than you will witness at any other time in your child's life.

Studies have shown that all forms of learning occurring at this stage are interconnected. This means that physical development is connected with emotional development, which is connected with intellectual development.

The young child is beginning to understand the world through relationship and language. 'Relationship' is a broad term, encompassing their relationship to themselves, to others and to the environment.

The 'terrible twos', as they are so awfully termed, is your child beginning to learn control over herself, in a search to define who she is. Personally, I've always found the threes to be harder than the twos. Gradually, they are learning about their own emotions and how to control them and what is an acceptable or unacceptable emotion – something heavily influenced by the culture in which they live.

Erik Erikson, a German psychoanalyst, put forward a theory about how people grow and develop emotionally. Erikson has had a major impact upon how we understand social and emotional development.

These years, he believed, were important for developing autonomy as opposed to shame and doubt. In simple terms, this means that as the child is developing they are coming across new situations and conflicts. As a result, delicacy is required in the caregiver's response. In an ideal world, the caregiver will be patient and encouraging, and will help the child gain a sense of independence and feelings of competency in their own abilities.

An overbearing and overprotective parent will prevent their child making mistakes and will solve problems for their child, leaving the child feeling inadequate – filled with self-doubt and shame.

The Swiss psychologist Jean Piaget became popular in the middle of last century when he developed a theory about how children's thinking develops. He understood children to be active participants in the world. They try to make sense of information.

Piaget described the ways of thinking that are characteristic of different age groups. At around the age of two, he said, the child moves to preoperational thought. He believed that the newborn was not capable of thought or language. Preoperational thought, in simple terms, means that the child is egocentric. That is, they are literally unable to see things from a different perspective, and as such their conclusions about life are based only upon what they can *perceive* rather than that which can be *reasoned*.

The Parent's Role

There are three main things the parent can do for a child of this age:

1. Help them develop independence – physically and emotionally

The ability to look after the body's needs, such as dressing and being able to go to the toilet independently, is highly important and can take some time to achieve. In developing these skills the child is learning fine-motor skills and self-care, and is developing autonomy.

The child is also learning about her emotions. Children are not mini adults and do not have the same control over their emotions. They need help. If you have a child who is an expert tantrum-thrower, teach her how to cope with her feelings in a way that is not destructive. Let her go into her bedroom and scream her head off. Let her punch her bed. Let her cry uncontrollably on the floor. These things are all right – she doesn't need to be smacked or told off for it. There are acceptable and unacceptable ways of expressing emotion. Kicking your brother in the face is not okay. Punching your mother is not okay. For these things there is a consequence.

Children at this age are as confused as the parent at the rawness and intensity of their feelings. Next time you see a child screaming hysterically, look in her eyes and you can often see terror there. It is as if they are frightening themselves. Your job is to help her while keeping your sanity.

Kalym was a toddler of extremes. When he was good, he was very, very good and when he wasn't – well, look out world! In a bookstore at the age of two, he was busy playing with a Thomas set in the children's area. When I said it was time to go he ran away from me screaming. In fact, the word 'screaming' does not do it justice. It was as if he was afraid of me, as though I was a child abuser attempting to hurt him. Every time I went near him, he would take off in the other direction, all the while screaming blue murder. Finally, an older woman picked him up and started talking to him, calming him down. I don't know who she was, but thank you to her. What was I meant to do? There was nothing I could do.

Almost every parent I know has one of these stories to tell. It's only my perspective that has now changed – I really don't care what other people think.

My priority is my child and getting us out of a situation unscathed. People who stare their disapproving stares – let them stare. It may seem as though the child is spoilt, but at the time the triggering event is beyond what anyone else can see. In the previous example, it was a Friday afternoon after a full week in childcare. Maybe Kalym was exhausted. Maybe he'd been pushed beyond what he could cope with. All that a parent can do is try to help them when they have these experiences. If it is at home, and it is the 10th morning in a row that the two-year-old has been whining for hours, give them a natural consequence of their behaviour. Put them in their room until they stop. If they are screaming and you can't cope, shut their door until you can. Go outside, put headphones on, do *anything* until you are in a position to help them. There will come a point eventually where their anger or other intense emotion will subside and they will need a cuddle and quiet cry. Let them. Sometimes I'm so emotionally raw from the experience that I'll cry too.

2. **Ensure that there is some time every day where the child is exposed to new experiences with the involvement of an adult.**

Note that I said an adult and also note that I said some time – do not read into this 'Mum should be at home with her child at all times of every day in order for the child to grow.' Spending time with an adult, and being able to have conversations with them, exposes the child to knowledge and language beyond that which they are presently capable. Older children can give the same benefit.

The adult helps the child in making sense of their world through such things as naming objects, describing sensations ('This glue is sticky') and making comparisons ('Do you want a big drink or a little drink?'). The number of things a child can learn in these situations is unlimited.

In terms of providing new experiences, a parent can do a million and one things, but don't get stressed out by this, just include them in what you are already doing:

* cooking ('that is hot, this is cold')
* going to visit friends or family
* doing the gardening (discover worms or an ant farm)
* hanging out the washing ('pass me the green peg')
* reading a new book

* going for a walk
* visiting local attractions – museums, zoos, farms and so on
* playing sport in the backyard
* helping light the fire
* doing the supermarket shopping.

These are just normal, everyday things that the child does with an active adult, someone willing to communicate and experience with them.

I am also a big advocate of creative pursuits, and try to incorporate these into daily life. I must admit, though, with my children at childcare, I feel somewhat relieved knowing that they are provided with artistic experiences every morning – another pressure off me.

A nursery rhyme a day

I am dedicated to nursery rhymes at this stage, as they are culturally and linguistically very important. They help provide a solid foundation for language. They are short and sweet, making memorisation that much easier. They are often nonsensical and just downright fun, encouraging both children and parents to play on words.

The purpose of this time (apart from the adult enjoying being with the child) is that it extends the child's present understanding of the world. It helps the child advance their understanding at their own pace. Gradually, they develop more and more confidence with skills and language until they master this knowledge. Then they are able to move on to something else. I cannot stress enough the amount of learning available to the child within normal everyday activities.

If, around now, you are a full-time working parent and are feeling guilty, don't. Studies have shown that the working parent can spend almost the same amount of 'active' time with their child as the stay-at-home parent. The stay-at-home parent may not converse or play with their child all day, but may instead try to keep them to one side, or drag them shopping or for a walk, and in doing so the child remains a life observer rather than a participant.

3. Back off and let them play

I can think of umpteen times when a parent has been visiting my house and chatting with me while their child is off with one of mine, or has found a toy and is contentedly playing. Worried that their child has been gone for so long, the parent goes in search of the wee explorer. Upon finding him, they do not leave him alone, but proceed to question him: What are you doing? Are you all right? What have you got there? It goes on and on.

What happens to the child? He is forced to stop playing and turn his attention to the adult who wants a verbal explanation of something that he quite reasonably cannot give. Eager to please, he makes up a parent-pleasing response.

Back off and leave them alone! If you're worried, quietly check on them and then go away.

Play is a child's attempt at making sense of the world, of reconstructing it in a way that makes sense to them.

Their imaginations are running wild, and they do not need an adult to come and help them. I learned this lesson from my mother, who was watching me one day when I was over at her house. Baby was fine, but there I was, in his face, talking and playing. She advised me to just leave him be so that he could learn that it was okay to play on his own.

There are some who say that play is becoming a lost art, and I have seen some evidence of this – children who need constant stimulation because they are unable to create their own experiences and entertainment. It is particularly evident as children become older and, rather than create their own games, they copy what they have seen on television. The importance of creativity in intellectual, personal and social development is so important that I dedicate a lot of time to it later in this book. For now, however, what needs to concern parents is *what* their child plays with. The first thing to do is forget all the claims made by toy manufacturers, that their toy will make your child more intelligent. Some toys are useful and some are rubbish.

Keep at the back of your mind that this age group is about forming relationships – with themselves, with others and with the world around them.

Don't buy toys that tell children how to play. These are usually the 'educational' toys. Then there are the toys that get major TV advertising time. They do one or two things, which the child masters (usually very quickly) and then shoves the toy in a corner never to be touched again.

SUITABLE TOYS FOR THE 1-4 YEAR OLD

* **Dress-ups** – they are exploring characters they have read or heard about as well as becoming other people they know.

* **Mini household items** – there are many cheap plastic toys available. I held the view for a time that providing mini items and allowing children to be involved in the household chores was enough for them. It wasn't until later that I've learned that they want their own normal-sized items which they can experiment and play with. They are imitating what they observe.

* **Dolls and stuffed toys** – these help children reverse their relationship with the adult, learning nurturing and empathy (even though dolly may be shoved upside down in the toilet).

* **Miniature items** – these include things like cars, trains, animals and so on. These remain incredibly popular and allow the child to create endless scenarios.

* **Construction items** – mini hammer and nail sets, blocks, scraps of wood, DUPLO®, mobilo® and so on.

* **Relationship toys** – these teach the child how things fit together and include such things as nesting cups, puzzles and shape sorters.

* **Sand and water toys** – there is so much activity going on in the sandpit or bath. Toys do not need to be expensive. You can use old plastic cups, sieves and saucepans from the kitchen.

* **Outdoor play** – these are toys that encourage gross motor-skill development, such as balls, bats, nets, hoops, bikes, tunnels, slides, swings and so on.

Other important things in the child's environment, although not deemed toys, include a library of quality books and suitable art supplies.

Ages 4-7

What's happening?

Another growth spurt takes place in the brain at around the age of four, adding even more neural connections and increasing the child's potential. With the first three years complete, the brain is like a canvas and a box of paints. The colours and potential are there, waiting to be used. The child now has an understanding of how the world works, how it is ordered and has established their emotional behaviours.

The biggest mistake made by parents and educators in the first three years is believing they must cram as much *knowledge* into the child as possible. Not so – the connections are formed through *experience*. Often our interpretation of knowledge is limiting – such as the belief that a child who reads early has a high IQ. The child may very well have a high IQ, but it is also quite possible for a child who cannot read by age four (or even seven) to have a high IQ.

Erik Erikson's child now moves to new emotional concerns. Erikson described children at this stage as balanced between learning initiative versus guilt.

The world begins to open up for children at this time, as their options, mentally and physically, expand. They become concerned with trying new things, such as bike riding, skipping, and investigating how sand and water can be manipulated. What they are doing is developing initiative – finding purpose in their activities.

If a parent considers them a nuisance and consistently tells the child to refrain from what they are doing ('Will you stop that noise!', 'Don't get those clean pants dirty!', 'Come inside – it's raining!') then the child is learning to become passive. They are learning to rely on someone else to tell them what to do and how to do it. In contrast, the parent who allows a degree of freedom in the home, with time and space for the child to indulge his interests, is helping him develop initiative.

For Piaget, the child is still working in the preoperational stage, seeing the world from an egocentric viewpoint. Perception is still important but now his judgements also involve intuition. This means that in understanding their world, the child will rely upon images rather than rules to make decisions. In other words, his thinking isn't always logical and he will rely on his intuition to solve problems. Intuition is both egocentric and ruled by perception.

> *A mother has a bag of lollies. She places a tall glass and a flat dish in front of the child. She tells the child to take a lolly and place it on her dish. When the child does this, the parent takes a lolly and places it in her glass. They take turns putting the lollies on the plate and in the glass until the lollies are all gone.*
>
> *The parent asks: 'Who has more lollies?'*
>
> *The child's response will be either: the parent, because her glass is taller, or the child, because her dish is wider.*
>
> *Either way, the child will base the answer on perception rather than logic.*

Children of this age will use whatever mental images they can over any form of logic.

They are very quick to give answers to even the most complex of questions because they manipulate the question until it fits in with their understanding of the world. Ask a child of this age why the sun stays up, and the response will be something like: 'Because it's awake', 'Because it is bright', or 'Because it's in the sky.'

The child will take two separate pieces of information and combine them to fit with their reasoning without finding it necessary for logic – something that Piaget called transductive thinking.

Because the child is still egocentric, it means that he is unable to see the world from a different person's perspective – in fact he may often be surprised to learn that the world is not exactly as he perceives it.

The Parent's Role

If we take on board all of the above information, we can get an idea of what a four-to-seven-year-old's world is all about – creativity, imagination, initiative and discovery.

It also means that children of this age literally cannot think logically. Now is not the age to expect your child to give a logical explanation for things they have done. Nor is it the age for you to provide them with logical explanations for why they should or should not do something.

You may logically explain why they cannot run out onto the road, but when their ball rolls onto the road, your logical explanations are forgotten. They only base their decisions on what they perceive.

We need to provide a safe environment for our children where they are able to explore and play, free from reprimands or overprotective adults.

It sounds easy enough, doesn't it?

In our house, we try to keep rules to a minimum:

* use your manners
* be gentle
* always tell the truth.

I have a real thing about manners, and there is an expectation that my children will use them. 'Please' and 'thank you' have been a part of their worlds since they were babes.

Being gentle encompasses how they are expected to treat themselves, other people and things around the house. They are young and boisterous, so rough-housing is a part of our life, but this can be done outside or within a defined area of the house.

I also have a thing about my children telling the truth. I expect it. However, I have to remember that, at this age, truth is subjective. I also know that my children have to feel safe enough to tell me the truth.

For me, the reason for truth is twofold. First, I cannot stand being lied to and appreciate honesty in my interactions with people. Life's a lot simpler when people tell the truth. Second, like many parents, I am sensitive to any form of abuse that my children may suffer. Being raised in the generation that was taught that one in four girls and one in 10 boys will be sexually abused, and that most abusers are people we know,

I have a real fear that this is something my children may go through. I am also aware of adult manipulation of children – 'This is our little secret.' or 'If you tell your mum or dad you'll get into trouble.'

I need my children to know that if any adult wants to share 'secrets' they are to come and tell me. I have to rely on their ability to tell me the truth.

SUITABLE TOYS FOR THE 4-7 YEAR OLD

Suitable toys for this age group are similar to those in the previous age group, but now there is greater emphasis on imagination and creativity.

* **Dress-ups** – put together a wonderful dress-up box with colourful pieces of material, hats, pegs, boxes and so on. Buying costumes can limit the child's imagination. A red cape, for example, can be Superman, Spiderman or any other superhero, but a Superman cape will always remain a Superman cape.

* **Art supplies** – give the child their own supply of art materials that they are responsible for looking after.

* **Percussion instruments.**

* **A portable CD or tape player** – preferably with a microphone. Give them a supply of tapes, both music and stories. With encouragement, children can give the greatest concerts at this stage, building their self-confidence.

* **Garden/nature** – children of this age group enjoy ant and worm farms, planting and growing vegetables and so on.

* LEGO® **and other construction toys** – blocks of wood, hammers and nails and other odds and ends, such as boxes, that they can use to build things.

* **Sporting equipment.**

A fairy tale a week

Having spent some time learning nursery rhymes, the parent of a four-to seven-year-old can now move on to fairy tales. These wonderful yet often horrific stories help the child in a number of ways – cognitively, she is learning how stories work; emotionally, she is learning some important life lessons. Carl Jung referred to the 'collective unconscious', which holds themes that are seen through all cultures and times. Fairy tales teach children about the archetypes of humanity – the eternal youth, the romantic, the tough exterior yet gentle-hearted man, the manipulative woman, and the innocent girl. These are all representative of people with whom we come in contact in our lives, and the fairy tale allows our child to develop a pre-understanding of them. Finally, fairy tales are a stimulus to the imagination. The stories are sometimes fantastical; many involve animals and provide background scenes to the child's play.

Fairy tales are fast on their way out, being replaced with television and PlayStation games that often depict random acts of violence and require no creative input from the observer.

Starting School

If the focus of the child of this age is on creativity, where does early teaching fit in? Why do we start our children at school at five?

It is important to make the distinction between the *focus* of the brain and the *potential* of the brain. It *is* possible to move directly to academic pursuits, such as learning to read. The focus on creativity does not mean that the child is not able to learn other disciplines. It means that the child is learning holistically, that is, by looking at the whole. For some people, this means that they change how they teach children to adapt to what the brain is doing. Because the creative side of the brain 'thinks' in circles and squiggles, for example, children will learn more quickly from a circular flashcard than a square one.

Early reading

Should we then be teaching our three- and four-year-olds how to read?

My response to this is: it depends. If we think of a child learning to talk, she does so because she is exposed to language. If a child is exposed at length to written language, she develops a natural inclination to learn to read.

If you have a child with a strong interest in learning to read, do not stop her on the basis that 'her brain is not meant to be doing this until later'.

Don't worry what other people think, be guided by your child.

When your child goes to school, it all becomes a moot point anyway, because literacy skills are a major focus of every new entrant classroom.

One of the best things we can do is help our child become ready for reading – and the best way to do this is by reading. Read to your child, read with your child, and listen to your child read.

While the latter may seem far-reaching, what your child will initially do is what they do with every new skill – they *pretend* to read. They look at the pictures and they make up a story to go along with them. And they are mighty proud of themselves when they do so.

All a parent needs to do is model reading behaviours, and encourage the child to use reading behaviours:

Before reading:

* hold the book the right way
* point to the title
* read the name of the author and illustrator
* discuss the cover – what do you think the book is about?

During reading:

* read from left to right and from top to bottom
* turn one page at a time
* discuss the pictures
* point to the words individually as you read
* notice punctuation
* recognise letters *and* the sounds that they make.

After reading:

* encourage your child to tell you what happened in the story
* relate the story to the child's personal experiences.

When the child starts school at the age of five, the parent becomes very important as a support person. The child will need to talk about what happens during the day as well as any emotional problems he is having settling in.

Schools can be intimidating places for parents because teachers are perceived as the experts in terms of our children. Yes, they may have specialised knowledge about a child's learning behaviours, but they are, like anybody else, limited by their own experiences and knowledge.

Teachers are evaluating and making judgements about your child based upon what they deem to be important.

No teacher knows your child as well as you do. When your child goes to school it does not mean that his or her teacher takes over the important role of parent.

Don't get bogged down by educational mumbo-jumbo. If you don't understand something, ask. That is your right as a parent.

Ages 7-11

What's happening?

A child of this age is a great inventor. She is able to integrate the information provided by the right brain and the two lower brains, and it is her intention to create what she perceives with her mind's eye.

She is beginning to be able to analyse her decisions at a detailed level. Before, she looked at the whole and made intuitive decisions; now, her reasoning becomes more logical as she is able to see things in a linear fashion. That is, she can see consequences more readily. This is the time when she will be introduced to the more 'academic' understandings of the world – science, maths, reading and writing.

During these years, Erikson believes that the child is balanced on the cusp of learning industry versus inferiority.

The child is concerned with how things work and how things are made. During these years of schooling, she has the opportunity to be rewarded for her industry. This is dependent upon positive reinforcement – her parents and teachers acknowledging, supporting and praising her efforts.

At the other extreme, the school system can also be a place where feelings of inferiority and inadequacy can arise. Too high an expectation on children, or blatant insults or ignoring a child's efforts result in these negative feelings.

The opportunity for success, therefore, is paramount at this age. This age group is still dependent upon external factors to make them feel good and to monitor their behaviour.

Children of this age are also beginning to gain an awareness of their own emotions and the emotions of other people. They begin to be able to identify their own internal world, and attribute their experience of it to the way they feel, rather than to what is happening in their environment. They can begin to control their emotions – therefore they are better able to *hide* their emotional state.

For Piaget, the child at seven moves into the concrete operational stage. She learns that there are certain rules that can be applied to

121

situations. These are mental, logical rules, rather than those that are perceived, and apply to *real* concrete objects. This means that she has difficulty looking beyond the here and now. Activities such as hypothesising or discussing the future are difficult for her to understand.

A parent shapes two balls of playdough of the same size and places them in front of the child and tells her that the balls are the same size.

Then the parent squashes one of the balls flat and asks the child, 'Which shape has the most playdough?' The child who has reached the concrete operational stage will be able to say that there is the same amount of playdough in each object. A child who has not reached this stage will say there is more playdough in the ball than the flattened shape.

A parent asks a child, 'Are there more boys or children in your class at school?' The child who has reached the concrete operational stage will say 'Children', whereas the child who has not reached this stage would say something like: 'There are more boys than girls.'

In doing this, she is showing that she is not yet able to manipulate parts to make a whole.

The child of this age is becoming less reliant on intuition and sensory observations while also becoming less egocentric. What she is now able to do is to take a concrete object and make it conform to certain rules.

The Parent's Role

Parents are now becoming less important in the child's world as peers start providing the child's self-esteem and feelings of belonging.

Their imaginations and belief in the world are running wild and they believe that all things are possible. I have heard many a parent say that this time is the golden age of their children's lives – they are usually independent but have not reached the confusion of the teenage years.

Maintaining the family

While it may seem like the best thing to do is to back off and leave the child to their own devices at this stage, maintaining a relationship with them is vital. They will still need time with their parents – *active* time. They will need to talk about what is going on at school and with their friendships. They will want to tell you about the world that they have created in their mind and show you their attempts at making this a concrete reality – their LEGO® construction, for example.

Building their self-esteem and defining life as a family is essential grounding for the later teen years.

Growing self-knowledge

The child of this age is really beginning to understand their individual talents and abilities. They know if they are in the bottom reading group or the top math group. They are more than able to compare their art with the other members of their class. The parent's job is to be as involved as possible in their child's education, without being dominating. If your child is struggling with reading in these years, ensure that something is being done about it – talk to your child's teacher. Educationally, these are the foundation years for high school, but children can still enter Year 9 not knowing how to read or write properly.

Gifts and talents

Parents also need to help their children make personal discoveries. They need to help them reflect on behaviour as well as helping them learn what they are good at.

If your child has a particular talent, support it as best you can.

In New Zealand we have a real problem with our Tall Poppies and talented children, and parents of those children can often feel isolated. We are afraid to label smart children as gifted, something I find absolutely absurd – why is it so bad to be smart?

If you have a particularly bright child, she is not necessarily

123

well-catered for within the education system. Government policy has changed – schools are now required to cater for the children at the upper end – but many schools are slow in making these changes. There *are* schools that do provide opportunities for these children, and if you are sending your child to one of these schools, you are lucky.

Not all children will find their gifts within the education system.

The child who spends hours and hours playing and constructing with LEGO®, for example, may not be able to define what he is good at, and this is okay too. The parent needs to accept the child for who he is and provide the environment for him to thrive in. You will only know these interests by talking to and observing him.

Parents also need to walk beside their children, helping them develop their independence, plan and organise their lives and learn to see the consequences of their actions.

Today's 'tweens' (pre-teens) are coming under more pressure to conform to a media-made ideal. Advertisers aim their marketing directly at these children, who are not earning money themselves, so that parents are under increasing pressure to provide what is so desperately *needed*. These 'life essentials' are usually short-lived fads and often very expensive. Encourage your children to do jobs around the house for pocket money so they can discover the true cost of all the things they 'need'.

Do not buy into any guilt traps – this is what the marketing executives are relying on.

During the Pokémon® phase a few years ago, my husband was teaching a Year 7 class who were obsessed with the associated merchandise – clothes, cards and so on. He decided to study these products rather than ban them. Within the unit of study, the class deconstructed the Pokémon® phenomenon. Initially they believed it to be part of a 'kid' world, a language they could speak that the adults couldn't. His purpose was to help them develop a more objective understanding of what was going on – that adults were behind it all – and they were swallowing their messages willingly. The result of these discoveries was that a large percentage of the class lost interest in the fad and moved on.

At home, a parent can help a child discover what they are being pressured into and to become more objective and discerning shoppers. Ultimately, this is encouraging the children to think for themselves – something they will need to do in the years to come.

Myths and legends

Having gone through nursery rhymes and fairy tales, now is the time for children to read and to hear myths and legends. In these stories the characters are not limited by our human physical constraints. Individuals have powers beyond that which can be observed. They are 'magical' in their abilities.

These stories appeal to this age group as they show the human potential in a way that cannot be observed. Children of this age instinctively search for heroes, and will find them wherever they can – even if it means a violent television or PlayStation character.

This search for heroes includes a search for real people who have gone beyond societal expectations.

If you do not provide heroes for your child, the media is happy to step in and do it for you.

The child will witness society's heroes – the musicians and actors – and will seek to imitate them. Far better for the parent to provide heroes who have helped shape humanity – the Einsteins, the Mother Teresas, the Martin Luther Kings and so on. If children were taught about these people at this age, it would fit perfectly with their biological drive to see the possibilities of all things.

SUITABLE TOYS FOR THE 7-11 YEAR OLD

Buying toys for this age group very much depends on the individual child and his or her interests. Just remember not to buy those toys that tell the child how to play, and don't get suckered-in by the latest television fad.

Creativity continues to be important so the child must have space and resources for this. Sport and music resources will need to be bought based on their interests and abilities.

Television should be limited, and I believe that PlayStations and machines like them have a very small place in the home – if at all. When you visit other people's houses, observe the different sorts of play in homes with PlayStations compared with those without. Those with PlayStation, often have their children inside on sunny days and, when it is switched off, mimicking what they have just played. Those homes without PlayStation will often see the children actively using their imaginations to create various worlds.

Ages 11-21

Youths 'have exalted notions, because they have not yet been humbled by life or learned its necessary limitations; moreover, their hopeful disposition makes them think themselves equal to great things – and that means exalted notions . . . All their mistakes are in the direction of doing things excessively and vehemently . . . they love too much, hate too much, and the same with everything else.'

ARISTOTLE

What's happening?

At this age, puberty has taken hold. Simply put, puberty is the period of sexual and reproductive maturity; it is a time of huge biological and hormonal changes.

The onset of adolescence is, as described by G. Stanley Hall in 1904, a period of 'storm and stress' – a view that has been supported by a variety of subsequent researchers. It is a time wrought with tension, rebellion, turmoil, over-dependence on peers and the battle between dependency and independence.

Joseph Chilton Pearce further explores the idea of the young person who is waiting for something great to happen. This adolescent ideal is well documented, and has been observed by many theorists. At this age, the young person has a feeling of greatness about himself; he feels the potential of the world. For Chilton Pearce, this biological pull has a purpose. He believes that in all probability we are meant to take the next evolutionary leap at this stage, using the frontal lobes of our brain. These frontal lobes were the last developed in evolutionary history. The social concerns of this age group are, according to Chilton Pearce, the drive that pushes us to want to contribute to society – to prove ourselves in the adult world.

The adolescent phenomenon of rebellion and reluctance to take part in adult society is comparatively recent. Such behaviour, according to Chilton Pearce, is the result of adults' lack of modelling and guidance. We are meant to be providing our young people with avenues of expression, of opportunities to explore their greatness. Instead, we place them in a kind of limbo – neither adult nor child.

Brain researcher Paul MacLean believed that adolescents should be moving towards a more humane and empathetic intelligence, which would open up at around age 15, provided that the necessary support structures had been put in place.

Erikson defines this time as a battle between identity versus role confusion. What the adolescent is doing is seeking to answer the question, 'Who am I?' Peers, sex, romance, career options and becoming an adult influence this developing perception of themselves.

Those who find it easier to move through this stage feel at home in their body, have a sense of direction and feel recognised and supported by the people who they count as important.

This is no small task for the adolescent. Their objective is to release their hold on childhood and gain a hold on adulthood. They begin to play with different roles – perhaps taking on a job – in order to come to terms with themselves. They are able to explore without having to commit to a final ideology, whether this is spiritual, vocational or in relationships.

Because the adolescent is trying on a variety of 'hats' he struggles to answer the important question of 'Who am I?' and becomes involved, as Erikson terms it, in role confusion.

In this state the adolescent is confused – he doesn't know where he is going, where he belongs or even who he is. Despite the negative emotion he will feel during this period, Erikson believes that such an exploration is both *necessary* and *beneficial*. This is because such explorations open up the world for the adolescent. If a 13-year-old designs his life path, and decides whom he will marry and what he will do for a career, then he is shutting off other possibilities.

In an effort for self-definition, this age group will attach themselves to an ideology – whether it is a mate, a peer group, a social, religious or political cause. Because they are struggling for self-definition, they look outside themselves for an answer. They then become overly attached and can be cruel in pushing away others.

For Erikson the fear of every adolescent is that they will never arrive at a place where they can answer the question, 'Who am I?' As such, every adolescent has the possibility of three negative traps:

* **Identity diffusion** – an unwillingness to commit adult life, that is, make a career or have a recognised place in the world.
* **Negative identity** – thinking poorly of themselves.
* **Deviant identity** – a lifestyle that is not regarded as valued and supported within society.

For Piaget, this time was representative of formal operations. In simple terms, this involves the ability to think in the abstract – to be able to make decisions and choices based on *thought* rather than *concrete evidence*. It is the ability to think about thinking.

While concrete operations involves the capacity to see all possibilities, formal operations means that the young person is now able to discern that *all possibilities are not created equal*. The adolescent, who has been relying on concrete operational thinking, will have begun to notice inconsistencies – some things are not certain, there are gaps in knowledge, there are contradictions. It is a time when the adolescent asks, not only if it is possible, but if it is the best choice.

This is the beginning of moral and ethical judgements. Left undeveloped, this results in behaviours that are based on building and creating more and more 'things'. It is now believed that there are many people who move into their adult years stuck in the concrete operations phase. Because of this, they are more selfish, materialistic and ultimately hold the potential for self- or world-destruction.

Now is the time for the young person to examine the knowledge upon which our world is based. At this stage of development, the adolescent requires *verification*. He requires explanations and reasons. Schools and tertiary institutions are excellent at catering for such things as scientific, technological and artistic knowledge. Cramming the young person's head with more knowledge will not, however, help him develop his formal operational thinking.

The new measurement for school success – NCEA – requires formal operational thinking, particularly in Year 13. The young people are not only required to reiterate knowledge that has been plugged into the short-term memory, but are also required to show abilities in problem solving, forming opinions, making evaluations, conducting investigations and making predictions.

This kind of abstract thinking is exactly what is needed at this age.

The Parent's Role

It is presently popular to stress the importance of the first three years of a child's life. It is important, but so is every stage of the child's development and growth. Children who seem happy and content at 10 can be rebellious and destructive by 14.

These tumultuous years until around 16 reflect the child doing what biology is urging him to – to enlarge his world by joining the group rather than being limited by the family. This age group has the answers and now the body to make choices, which is very scary for the parent, who cannot be there at all times and must let them go. All that the parent can do (apart from lock them up) is to try to be there as much as they are allowed, to step in if necessary and to try and keep the child's view of the world a broad one.

Many parents view these years as the hardest on the parenting journey.

> *Nothing prepared me for the change in my daughter. One day we were best friends and the next she hated me. I had to make decisions – like whether or not she was allowed to go to a party or what time she'd have to be home – and she hated me for that.*
>
> Bobby

Parental stresses:

* loss of control over child's behaviour
* advice falling on deaf ears
* adolescent pushing away from parent
* the adolescent's need to seek independence
* fears for adolescent's safety
* disapproval of choices
* not knowing what is going on in their young persons' life
* tertiary education expenses
* unfinished chores – school and home
* dissatisfaction within the parents' marriage (this gets better when the teen leaves home).

Before you decide to run away from home and not return until your young person is 21, take solace in the fact that the turmoil that your adolescent goes through does not have to be the stress and storm many would have us believe it is.

The fact is, you can and do make a difference not only in how well they fare during these years, but also in the choices they will make in their adult years. The way you parent counts.

Acceptance and encouragement

At this stage of their development, the young person is observing the world around them, and beginning to understand the fallibility of adults and other societal structures. This is a tentative time, when the parent needs to encourage their child's questioning attitude, as the answers that they find at this time may follow them long into adulthood. The amount of satisfaction or dissatisfaction that they find in the world will influence the decisions they make. They have a perception, formed since their early years, about whether the world is a good or a bad place.

During these years, the young person has inherent belief in their invincibility – even immortality – and is therefore prone to make decisions that are risky and potentially dangerous. The parent can serve to help guide these feelings in a positive direction. In their idealistic view of the world, and their feelings of huge personal potential, the parent who can stand beside their young person and support them in their feelings of greatness is doing them a favour.

Unfortunately, adults often force the young person of this age to conform to a materialistic definition of life, that is, the adolescent must take on a particular job or receive particular training in order to earn money. Their ideals are squashed, their questions ignored or even punished, and they are forced either to completely rebel against the world or to conform to its rules.

A person of this age feels strongly about things, whether or not they are accepted by the adults around them. Your responses to their behaviour help them decide what kind of person they are, and whether or not they are valued.

If they feel rejected and belittled, they take away negative feelings about themselves.

Keep involved in their world

When allowed, a keen interest and involvement in the changing world of the adolescent means that a parent has greater influence over the decisions they make. While the young person is fighting for their independence, the need for the parent to remain involved is very apparent. Watching school productions or watching them play sport is a way of showing support.

While the family home may change into a place dominated by teens, with the pantry always empty, the open-door policy for friends means that you get to know the peers your young person has chosen. It also means that your home becomes a place where your teens can be themselves – a place where they belong, an important feeling at this age.

Keep communication going

There is a time and a place for talking. Be sensitive to the moods of your teen (and they will be swinging) and keep on talking – and, more importantly, *listening.*

Communication is also physical. No need to stop the hugs – the teen needs them, and so does the parent.

Keep a wide social group

This is a very social time for children, who feel the strong urge to belong to their culture. Unfortunate is the child whose only point of reference is belonging to their peers. Friends, cousins, uncles, aunts and grandparents all provide a different mirror for the teen. If you have a broad yet close-knit set of friends who the teen feels valued and accepted by, it opens the doors for more opportunities. You may not be able to understand or give advice about a particular problem or need, but another close adult might. Such a network will decrease the risk of the adolescent needing to attach himself too strongly to the ideologies discussed above. If he already belongs to a wide social group, that reduces the need to look outside for religions, partners and negative social groups.

This age group is marked by their group mentality and their idealised, golden view of society. Disappointed with the society that we adults have provided them, they begin to create their own, based on their ideas of what should or might be.

Cultural belonging is far broader and ultimately more important than peer belonging. This social development, which began at around the age of seven and revived at age 11, is the biological urge to step out on one's own into society.

Support spiritual, philosophical and moral explorations

In these years, the adolescent will be likely to explore spirituality, philosophy and morality. With hormones running rampant, these young people also feel an urge to have sex. Again, they receive mixed messages: television and media images say that sex is adult and okay, while religious beliefs and/or parents say that such feelings should be ignored or, in extreme cases, are wrong. In developing formal operations, the young person begins to be able to make decisions about sex and drugs. Stuck in the concrete operations phase, he will make decisions based on what is right in front of him. This means that if he goes to a party and is offered drugs and/or alcohol, he will more likely be excessive in his experimentation and not be able to see the longer-term consequences. By being able to think in the abstract, he knows that not all choices are equal.

Those things which my generation got up to in adolescence are now happening earlier and earlier. Alcohol, drugs and sex are choices that 10-, 11- and 12-year-olds are saying 'yes' to.

A few months ago I had a long chat with around fifteen 11- and 12-year-olds. They openly chatted with me about getting drunk and smoking dope. I was fascinated with their perceptions of sex. They believed (thanks to Bill Clinton?) that being sexually active did not involve oral sex. Oral sex was okay, while penetration was not.

Note: these were not naughty or neglected young people.

The parent who has moved into and hopefully beyond formal operations can serve as their adolescent's support person.

At all times we should encourage adolescents to seek answers from adults beyond their parents.

The parent does not provide the answers, but supports the questions and the process to reach decisions.

The questioning mind combined with the development of moral and ethical values means that the young person is seeking answers to the wider world questions. During this search, it is common to become disenchanted with the world. Indeed, this particular journey fills books and movies. The trust and idealism of youth fails in the face of hypocrisy and lies. The adult world appears nothing like they thought. In both their idealism and egocentricity they can believe that they have the *right* and the *ability* to change the world.

It is at this time that religious dogma can alienate the adolescent from the adult. I shall use the example of Christianity, only because of my personal experiences. The adolescent will begin to examine the foundations upon which he was brought up, and this includes religious beliefs. Upon examination of the Bible, he will find contradictions, differing opinions and ultimately (hopefully) begin to question whether the book was divinely inspired. Without this personal investigation the adolescent will either rebel completely against the Bible, or conform without question. The person who chooses the latter is obvious in the way he talks about his views – rather than thinking through his beliefs, he takes on those which are handed to him, often engaging in black-and-white thinking while being very judgmental of other people.

The young person who is allowed and even encouraged to question the foundations upon which his family and society live is ultimately going to be a stronger and higher-level thinker. The adolescent may uncover all sorts of information with regards to his religion and may return to it with a fuller understanding, or they may move on from it completely.

Make the transition to adulthood easier by defining it

'Adolescent' is a popular term used to define a group of people who are too old to be children and too young to be adults. Historically, the transition to adulthood was clearly defined by rites of passage. These rites served as a social and internal symbol that the young person had moved to the next phase of life.

Modern-day rites will provide the child/adult with specific under-standing of their changing societal role with increased responsibility and rights.

Ages 21+

What's happening?

If not all people reach their capacity to move into formal operations, even fewer reach beyond it. It was once believed that the capacity for brain development did not move beyond what it was in adolescence.

The young adult, according to Erikson, is coming to terms with intimacy versus isolation.

Intimacy involves the ability to form close friendships and relationships without giving up one's own identity. In forming intimate relations, there will always be the risk of rejection – an emotionally painful ordeal. The fear of rejection can result in the young adult forming shallow relationships – a form of self-protection.

For Piaget, formal operations is the final stage of intellectual development.

Around 40 years ago Bruner put forward the idea that there would come a time when it would be acknowledged that there was a further stage of development beyond adolescence. From this theory evolved the development in the 1970s of post-formal operations – a theoretical framework that has continued until today. This arose because Piaget's fourth stage did not encompass the wider adult characteristics of society. Such a view has since been widely explored and accepted. The adult does not think like an adolescent, nor like a child.

Where adolescents are problem *solvers*, those in the post-formal stage are problem *finders*. This fifth stage of development includes such things as wisdom, the understanding and acceptance of the paradoxical nature of life, the ability to understand that one holds a subjective view of life – as do all people – and that therefore it is acceptable for another person to have a different and yet equally valid point of view.

The post-formal thinker will also move from theoretical postulations to applying that understanding in real-world situations, showing the ability to live by that which they believe. They will develop morally and spiritually, guided by views such as the individual rights of all people. They will also have a universal life perspective, resulting in a more empathetic, ecological and non-materialistic view of life.

At this stage of development, the adult accepts and welcomes new information and challenges – knowing that his views are subjective and therefore fluid and open to change.

The Parent's Role

While it is a commonly held myth that parents have no role in the lives of their adult children, most people will acknowledge the importance of a continuing relationship with their parents. The parent is there to assist the young adult in her journey by observing, supporting and sharing.

Increasingly common is the idea of the eternal youth, the adolescent who never grows up. More young adults return to their family home, spend their time in self-centred and instantly gratifying pursuits and spend their money on ever-more expensive toys. There are many theories about why this is happening, but regardless of these, the parent needs to encourage the young adult in her journey – to take responsibility for her actions and to develop a wider-world view.

To cater to their adolescent behaviour while they are at an age that warrants adult behaviour does young people a major disservice.

There may be difficult decisions for the parent to make. I, for example, having left home at 17, moved back home with my parents at 23 with a child in tow. I am very grateful that they allowed me to do this. At all times, however, the understanding between us was that this was temporary, that I would move on from them. Their support at this time was essential for the future of both my son and myself.

Similar decisions may be required from the parent who learns their offspring is addicted to drugs or suffering from a mental illness. Rather than resume the role of controller, it is better to walk beside them and to encourage healing and integration back into society. It is essentially up to the individual parent how much they will give their child in the adult years – financially and emotionally.

I believe the rule of thumb would be to help just enough so that she is not suffering and just enough so that she is encouraged towards independent thought and responsibility.

Code SEVEN

THE OLD CODE: Genius

I talked in the first section about the Child Genius Syndrome, where the message that every child is the next genius is drilled into us. At the same time, we carry our humble Kiwi attitude with us, where it is not okay to talk about the great things our kids are doing for fear of skiting or making someone else feel small.

The New Zealand education system can give the same message:

> *My daughter's school has a policy of not giving grades for achievement. They give a grade for effort but then there is no comparison for her academic work. They say that it shouldn't matter what other people are achieving, all that is important is how she is doing against herself. I find the idea idealistic and unrealistic. I need to know if she is doing well, or if she is behind for her age. How can I help her if I don't know?*
>
> Maureen

> *When my daughter started school they gave her a whole series of tests. When I went to parent/teacher interviews I came away feeling so inadequate. She hadn't performed very well and I felt like I should have been educating her a lot more than I ever bothered – or even felt the inclination to do before she started school.*
>
> Melanie

Education has undergone a big turn-around from competition-based learning and achievement towards one of cooperation. The latest curriculum framework encourages a balance of both of these traits, and individual schools interpret and implement the document as they see fit. In some junior sports, scores are not taken during games, so that no one feels like a loser. However, in other schools academic achievement is very important from an early age.

If a teacher tells you that your child is achieving at Level 3 in English, do you know what it means? Is that good or bad? Is she behind? Is she advanced? Does it matter?

While it may be 'politically correct' to say that it doesn't matter, we all know that it does.

The Genius Industry

Let's look for a moment at the billion-dollar child-genius industry. This is based on the concept that your child, given the right environment and experiences, will become the next Einstein or da Vinci. And so, when our children walk and talk at the normal age, we feel guilty because we've been taught that they could – and should – be doing better.

Next time you are in a toy store, have a look at all the advertising that is directed at this insecurity. Play has taken second place to education. If a toy is advertised as educational, then it must be better for the child.

Sound ludicrous? It is.

Children are learning all the time. They learn through observation and interaction with their environment. It is impossible to separate time between learning and not learning. They are learning as they play, as they eat, as they trash the kitchen cupboard, pulling out the saucepans and making a band. They do not need bright flashing lights and classical music to learn.

One example is the million-dollar international company that is based on the theory known as the Mozart Effect. In 1993, a group of researchers published a report in the journal *Nature* that said that they had proven that listening to Mozart improved spatial reasoning. Their methodology was to expose three different American college groups to different conditions before getting them to sit a standardised test involving spatial reasoning. One group listened to 10 minutes of Mozart's music; another sat in silence; the third listened to relaxation music. The first group performed the best in the test.

Many researchers have viewed this experiment as flawed and more recently, in an article published in *Psychological Science* in 1999, Doctor Kenneth Steele stated that in the experiments he and his co-workers conducted, they could not find any causal link between listening to Mozart and performance.

The same group of researchers who conducted the initial

investigation examined three- and four-year-olds' spatial-reasoning ability. And what was their conclusion? That after eight months, those children who had keyboard lessons were better able to put together puzzles compared with the groups that were given computer lessons and singing lessons, and with the control group which was not given any lessons.

My response: *so what?*

Does this mean that I should force my children to have keyboard lessons so that they can put together a puzzle faster? No! We have a keyboard at our house and the children often play on it. Tony plays well and sits with them, making music, because he feels the inclination at the same time they do. Imagine the difference if it was a requirement to be at that keyboard.

The Mozart Effect is now worth millions of dollars. There are videotapes, music tapes and flashcards. It is fascinating how a little bit of information can become 'fact'; the consumer believes it and spends the money. Under the guise of developing a child genius, a parent can spend around $30 on a special CD of Mozart's music. Or (if they really want to test this theory), they can go into any second-hand music store, or even the bargain bin at The Warehouse, and find Mozart's music for a couple of dollars.

We take our child's intelligence, or lack of it, personally. Even the parent who claims it doesn't matter gets that glimmer in his or her eye when describing something that their child can do really well.

Yep, I do it too. Damn, that was hard to admit.

The chapter on Code Six looked at the consequences of forcing our children to be too sophisticated too early. Now we come to the consequences of having an underlying belief in the genius of each and every child.

Such a belief sets us up to be disappointed in our children. It makes us focus on their intellectual development at a very early age, and in looking for 'traditional' genius it is very likely that we miss the gifts that our child actually has. If our child loves to spend hours playing with LEGO® or hunting for ants or splashing in water, we can be made to feel that we are depriving them of an opportunity to develop their genius – a supposed right and expectation of every child today.

While it may be a nice ideal, let's chuck the code of Genius into that trusty obsolete bin and look to a new code that will help us help the child we have – let's encourage their flair!

THE NEW CODE: Flair

In trying to define intelligence, I asked my seven-year-old son Kalym whether he was smart. He replied that he was. I then asked him what being smart meant. His nose wrinkled and his eyes squinted in thought.

What followed went something like this:

'Well, Mum,' says he, 'I think there are two things that make someone smart.'

'What are they?'

'First of all, a smart person tries new things. And the second thing is that they get lots of things right.'

How refreshing to have a child's ability to cut through the crap and find the simple truth. In his simple terminology he defined the importance of both intellectual and creative thought. Without one, the other is only half of its potential.

When we think of intelligent individuals we can see that they are those who are able to think of alternatives, to 'think outside the square'. We think of societal icons as well as the woman down the road who has done her own interior decorating with style and flair. We think of Einstein, van Gogh, Ernest Rutherford, Colin McCahon, Sam Neill and Jane Campion. We can describe each of these people as highly creative *and* highly intelligent, in very different ways.

It is often tempting to focus on a particular trait – such as artistic flair, the ability to be self-expressive or to possess a high IQ. But if our objective for our children is to have them grow into healthy, contributing members of society who are capable of appropriate self-expression and who are working at their potential, then the approach that we take to raising them should be *holistic*. The term holistic implies, quite simply, the need to keep the whole child in mind.

Skills, Knowledge and Talent

Intelligence is a delicate mix that in order to flourish must encompass skills, knowledge and talent. People of intelligence have a strong foundation of all three of these traits appropriate to their particular area of endeavour. High intelligence in the sciences is taking the known to the unknown; in the arts it is the creation of an expression. I can stamp my feet to express my anger, or I can delve into colour and form in the creation of a piece of visual art. It is not difficult to know which requires greater capacity.

Letting your child guide you

One approach to intelligence originated with the American psychologist Dr Howard Gardner and his theory of Multiple Intelligences. Gardner postulated that intelligence was not for single measurement and that standardised IQ tests were inadequate for measuring the potential and capacity of intelligence.

Each of the areas of intelligence presented by Gardner can be developed to a high and *creative* level. It involves the utilisation of both the left and right hemispheres of the brain. We tend to focus on one particular side, but it would seem to make greater sense to develop both sides of the brain.

TYPES OF INTELLIGENCE

Gardner initially outlined seven types of intelligence, which are now generally accepted in the educational, psychological and scientific communities. These seven intelligences are listed below.

* **Linguistic:** language-smart – poets and novelists.
* **Logical/Mathematical:** being good at mathematics.
* **Musical:** rhythm, tone and pitch.
* **Bodily/Kinesthetic:** being body smart – athletes, dancers and actors.
* **Spatial:** being able to visualise and construct things in your mind – pilots, sailors, chess players, artists and scientists.
* **Interpersonal:** being able to communicate well with other people.
* **Intrapersonal:** understanding and controlling oneself.

While Gardner's ideas seemed revolutionary to the education and scientific community, really he just gave labels to what the average parent is already quite able to observe within their own children when they come to realisations like: 'My child is good at art.'

The fact that the scope of intelligence is now wider is excellent for those parents of children who were previously unaccepted and/or not catered for within the mainstream education system. Some schools have changed their entire ideology to fit with Gardner's theories. For example, at Matahui Road School in Katikati, every topic of study involves each of the intelligences, so that the children have an opportunity to develop all their intelligences while being able to find success in their particular area of strength.

Since labelling these intelligences in his 1983 book *Frames of Mind*, Gardner has continued to explore the meaning and types of intelligence.

In 1999 he published *Intelligence Reframed*, examining the potential for other kinds of intelligence – spiritual, moral, existential and naturalist. Naturalist intelligence, that is, being nature-smart – being sensitive to plants, animals, rocks and so on – is, Gardner says, as worthy as the original seven intelligences. People who use this type of smart include farmers, zoologists, veterinarians, herbalists and geologists.

He wrote about the importance of existential intelligence – the ability to ask profound questions about life and death. Philosophers and artists have this capacity. He could not however, pinpoint an area of the brain from which such a capacity evolved, so it was not, at this stage, given the 'full' treatment of the other seven.

What Can a Parent Do?

Know your child

This is a seemingly obvious suggestion, but it is important to become an expert in the nature, needs and talents of your child. This is particularly important when the child is very different from the parent.

Observe

One of the best ways of knowing your child is to observe them in action. Experts train for years to be able to make an observation of a child. For our parental purposes, however, we are already well ahead of any specialist. This is because we already spend so much time with our children, and rely on both left- and right-hemisphere thinking in our observations.

Our own intuitions and holistic view of our child are probably fairly accurate.

We see our children in a variety of contexts, and observing them in their own environment helps us understand them in their world.

Observing children can be as complex or as simple as time and inclination allows. Some adults find it difficult to sit back and just watch a child, particularly a young one. They rush to fill in the gaps, to prevent any accidents or to seek explanations for actions. Observing children requires that the parent join the child's world at her level, free from judgement or pressure.

Journals

Keeping a written record of your child is an excellent way of gaining a fuller understanding, and it will become a treasure in later years. Many 'baby journals' or 'baby books' are sold in stores based on this premise. They are often, however, overly directive about what to write – for example, baby 'firsts' such as Christmas or birthdays or medical conditions. These can be useful, but a self-created journal, placed in a ring binder, will probably work best so that pieces can be added as required – including works of art, photographs and stories. When you are too busy to add to it for six months, you'll not feel any guilt because you haven't filled in the correct spaces.

The work of Vivian Gussin Paley is of particular interest. It involves extensive observation and recording of children in their kindergarten years. She has an amazing ability to use conversations and stories of children in order to gain a better understanding of them in their world. At an age ripe with fantasy, children, through their language, give insight into what they perceive as important, bringing things to a conclusion that makes sense to *them* regardless of any interference from adult logic.

If you choose to have a ring binder to fill with observations of your child, don't get too hung up on doing it right. It doesn't have to look like a work of art with fancy borders and headings.

IDEAS OF THINGS TO INCLUDE IN YOUR JOURNAL:

* watching your child at play and recording what he or she does
* conversations with friends
* conversations you have with your child
* photographs
* artwork
* certificates or any achievements they gain

* stories they have dictated to you or, as they get older, ones they have written themselves
* funny or special moments.

Labels

Some parents, in order to understand their child, seek labels for them from educationalists, psychologists or other medical professionals. To understand personality, they may look at books about temperament and decide that little Sally is melancholy. It may explain her behaviour at certain times.

Another book may talk about the way a child receives information, and the parent can then label their child as a kinesthetic, visual or aural learner.

Still another book will teach that different children need different kinds of affection in order to know they are loved.

I have read many of these books with interest, seeking the answers to explain some behaviour or another. I have had moments of 'Aha!' when I see a description for one child – but then I turn the page and find another (just as suitable) label for the same child. Dispositions, temperaments and learning styles are interesting, but in my experience they do not stand the test of time.

Children are complex and ever-changing creatures who rarely settle under a particular label for any major period of time. Personally, I cannot rely on these labels to give me a sense of predictability about their behaviour. Far better, I believe, is to do your own observing and come to your own conclusions, relying on your gut instinct and own intelligence to understand your child.

Observing intelligence

In terms of intelligence, observing your child can tell you many things. Most importantly, it can give you information about the child's natural inclinations.

How your child chooses to spend her undirected, free time will give clues as to where her talents and motivations lie.

Given the opportunity, what would your child most prefer to do? Does she want to be outside playing with balls and bats? Does she beg you to let her paint or draw? Does she play with dinosaurs? Does she devour every book in sight? More than likely, your child will combine a number of interests, depending upon environmental influences such as the weather and whether she has had enough sleep the night before. Her interests and activities will also change as she grows.

If we return to Gardner and his different types of intelligence, we can draw conclusions about what kind of smarts our individual child has. These are brief summaries, as there are entire books and tests available to find the dominant intelligence, but an overview is really all a parent needs, as it can often be quite obvious and something that we already intuitively know.

CHOOSING ACTIVITIES YOUR CHILD WILL ENJOY

Linguistic-intelligent children enjoy:

* reading books

* listening to stories – tapes, CDs and other people

* writing – stories in a diary or journal

* talking

* playing word games such as I Spy and Scrabble, crosswords and word finds.

Logical/Mathematical-intelligent children enjoy:

* doing brainteasers

* playing with calculators

* making lists, organising information – helping with the grocery shopping

* using computers

* making or solving codes.

Musical-intelligent children enjoy:

* singing
* playing an instrument
* composing music
* playing with sound
* listening to music.

Kinesthetic-intelligent children enjoy:

* playing sport
* building models
* doing puzzles
* performing – either acting or dancing
* playing dress-ups.

Visual/Spatial-intelligent children enjoy:

* using computers
* using video and still cameras
* doing art
* make-believe activities
* decorating their own bedroom.

Interpersonal-intelligent children enjoy:

* communicating – discussing ideas, giving and receiving feedback, interviewing
* teaching
* acting
* socialising
* helping other people.

Intrapersonal-intelligent children enjoy:

* keeping a journal or diary
* spending time alone
* working on their own interests, in their own time
* having personal space within the home
* reading and learning about thinking, concentration and metacognitive issues.

This general overview gives you some clues as to what kind of intelligence your child may possess. Some children are particularly focused on one, while others may have developed all of the intelligences. Most children will have a combination of two or three.

Having observed your child, it is just as important to communicate with them. When you have a conversation with them, or are playing a game, you can learn what kinds of things come easy to them and what kinds of things they find harder. Don't rely on other people to tell you what type of child you have. School tests and teacher observations may give you a wider perspective, but they are far from definitive.

Trust your instincts and own intelligence but at the same time do not ignore educational evidence that may be contrary to what you believe.

Believe in your abilities as an educator.

Many parents feel comfortable with themselves in the parenting role, but the idea of also being a child's educator can be threatening.

We believe that there are teachers and systems in place to look after the intellectual development of our children. In some circumstances, this is accurate. Many children have their needs met within the education system, but there are many who do not. There are many things that influence this: the nature and talents of an individual child, a particular teacher in a given year and the school that your child attends. Once your child hits five and is in the care of other adults for six or more hours a day, your role as educator has not finished. Children are far more individualistic than the mainstream education allows for, and it is unrealistic to expect that a single teacher can meet all the needs of some 20–30 students.

Through regular interactions with your child's teacher, you will (hopefully) know that your child is acquiring both the knowledge and skills that will see them into their adult, working, creative life. Success, however, is also dependent upon things such as *attitude* and *motivation*.

It is the parents' role as educator to help a child become a discerning, objective and independent thinker. I have already discussed the message of conformity within education. This conformity is quite reasonable – there needs to be a base line from which all children can venture out into the world – but, as a parent, you must choose if you want to go above and beyond this base line. If you do, there are schools that encourage success and independent thought. If you do not have access to one of these, then the onus is on *you* to be an educator.

Essentially, the parent is there to support, to motivate, to question and to mentor. If your child is interested and/or skilled in an area where you are not, find someone who is. If they outgrow that person's knowledge, find someone else to fill the gap.

You need to help your child gain skills or knowledge in the areas in which they are naturally talented. If it is science, extend them in this area; if it is sport, extend them; if it is art, music, or writing, extend, extend, extend. If you don't do this, it is unlikely that anyone else will, and their gift will lie latent – potentially for years.

The important point in gaining knowledge is the way in which it is presented. If a child learns in a fixed, muted environment where they are not encouraged to explore ideas or develop original thought, then she is unlikely to try and push the boundaries at a later stage.

For example, take a scientist: if she passively takes on board what she learns, believing in its ultimate truth, then she will see no need for reaching beyond what is currently known.

Creativity is innovative, and without knowing truth as an interpretive understanding one can't look with freshness upon one's own area of endeavour.

Cutting off the heads of our Tall Poppies

There are two different ideologies influencing parents in our society. In the first, we have parents who want their children to peak at a very young age: they put extraordinary amounts of pressure on their young ones to perform at a high level in all areas. In the second, parents observe the talents of their children but fear that if they nurture or talk about their child's intelligence they are boasting. This latter ideology is the Tall Poppy Syndrome.

It is particularly prevalent in the area of academic intelligence. We depend upon teachers to tell us if our child is intelligent and have an expectation that the work they are given is aimed at their particular academic level. This may be true in some circumstances, *but not all*. If you have an academic child, celebrate him and realise that you need to support him at home. It doesn't mean that you are pushing him or putting undue pressure on him. In fact, it is highly likely that he will thrive when faced with the challenge.

There are children (most of them, I would guess) who do not have a particular area where their talent shines. More than likely their unique gift will be in the combination of talents they possess. These are the children who do pretty well in most areas but do not perform in any area to the level of excellence. For these children, school will provide the knowledge and experiences that they require, but it would be a mistake to assume that their uniqueness will be acknowledged and supported. As the parent, you will know what your child is like, and the best thing you can do is have an expectation of success and continue to provide an environment that supports higher-level thinking – questioning, independence, sensitivity, exploration, direction and so on.

The child, for example, who performs at an average level in writing may spend hours at home creating his own stories or poems. Go with this – get him a special notebook or encourage him to type his own stories and design covers for them.

You may have a child who loves to talk and perform at home and yet doesn't make the lead in the school play. So what? Give him the scope to indulge his interests at home.

In order to nurture the nature of your individual child or children, there are practical steps that you can take outside the mainstream school system. If I ran the education system I would abandon generalised homework altogether in favour of allowing children the opportunity to develop their own strengths, particularly in the primary school years when many teachers give homework for the sake of homework rather than to encourage any real learning.

THE SIX-STEP APPROACH TO NURTURING YOUR CHILD'S INTERESTS

1. Talk

Knowing your child, sit down and have a chat about things that he is interested in. Find out what it is that he likes doing best, and what he wishes he could do more of. His answers may surprise you, and you need to be okay with whatever response you get – show no signs of disappointment. In doing this, you are assured that he is personally involved and motivated. You are also ensuring that he feels accepted and encouraged for his interests and talents. Talk about what he likes or is interested in. It could be a sport (tennis), art (painting), or an idea (Why do I have to go to school?), a topic (dinosaurs) or an activity (cooking). Any of these things are just fine. Share your own experiences or those of other people you know and encourage your child to do the same.

2. Set goals

Through your discussion, ascertain what it is your child would like to be able to do in their particular area of interest. Does he want more knowledge? To create something? To reach a particular skill level? As the parent you can share ideas, particularly if he cannot think of any ideas. If he likes painting, for example, he may not know what it is he would like to do except paint. If you need inspiration for how to develop his interests, visit the local library, surf the Internet, or check out the local toy or book store. You are bound to get some great ideas, and your child will say, 'Yes! That's what I want to do!' This isn't necessarily a short process, and may take a week or two of reading, watching and exploring before he will reach this point.

3. Make a plan

When he has an idea of something he wants to do, that he finds both interesting and challenging, work out what you are going to need to do in order to help him get it. You may have to purchase something (such as a telescope), make regular visits to the library, take a trip somewhere, or provide space and time for him to explore his ideas within the home. You will need to keep the ideas realistic, because only you know what your financial and time restrictions are.

4. Implement the plan

Having put in the hard yards in terms of time and possibly money, now is the time to let go and watch him fly. If you have put pressure on him to pursue a particular area that he doesn't have a *real* interest in, you will find that he does not want to spend the time doing what he said he wanted to do. I can follow this kind of process with seven-year-old Kalym, and once he's come to a decision he will be up first thing in the morning and working on his project as soon as he comes home from school – and sometimes well into the night. This kind of motivation is not the 'norm' for him, as I struggle to get him to complete homework and he can be troublesome when bored (what child can't?). At this stage, the parents' role is encouraging, questioning and supporting their child.

5. Evaluate and celebrate

There will come the time when the child has either completely lost interest in his project or has achieved what he set out to do. This may be weeks – or months – later. Be led by the child. Now is the time to celebrate what he has done – talk, watch, take a photograph, read or taste – whatever it may be. Make a big deal if he has achieved what he wanted, and if he tried several different things but couldn't do them, then make a big deal of the process that he went through to get to that point.

6. Begin again

Finally, it's time to begin the process all over again. He may want to continue exploring the same area, or try something completely new. Either way is fine.

Know the Education System

Many parents still think of schooling as it was in their day. Changes in education are happening all the time. You can't assume that certain topics are or are not being covered, or that there are certain expectations being met, unless you actually *know* what is going on inside your child's classroom, the school and the education system as a whole.

Trends occur in education, and as one phases out another takes its place, or new names are devised to describe the same thing. It can be tricky trying to keep up with it all.

The New Zealand education system has gone through massive change since the early 1990s when the entire curriculum was rewritten. More recently, we have seen School Certificate and Bursary give way to NCEA. Each step of the way has been fraught with conflict – some schools accusing the government of dumbing down the curriculum and choosing to have their pupils sit exams from outside New Zealand. Other schools make full use of the opportunity to personalise their NCEA programmes.

We've also been bombarded with claims that the education system is failing our boys. A basic understanding of how the system works is necessary for every parent in order to have a real knowledge of what their child is doing at school. What follows is an overview of the current curriculum that exists in most New Zealand schools.

Early childhood

New Zealand early childhood centres are founded upon the educational policy document *Te Whariki*. It is based upon four key areas: empowerment, holistic development, relationships, and family and community. Within each of the four areas, there are five key areas of learning: wellbeing, belonging, contribution, communication and exploration.

The scope of the document is such that a variety of educational approaches can be used, so different centres will have different philosophies, such as Montessori, Steiner, Reggio Emilia, Project and so on.

Primary and secondary education

The official policy for New Zealand education is the New Zealand Curriculum Framework.

Figure 1

Figure 1 is a simple, visual representation of the curriculum, taken from the New Zealand Curriculum Framework document. The Principles refer to the school subjects, each of which have their own documents which outline the 'strands' to be taught within each area. The Essential Skills must be developed within each of the learning areas. Subject areas apply from Level One through to Level Eight.

Figure 2 on the following page is taken from the mathematics curriculum document. If you are told that your Year 4 pupil is working at Level Two in math, then you know that she is at an average level. If she is working at Level One, then you know that she is not doing so well, at Level Three she is doing better than average, and so on. Each subject area has a similar chart. Knowing and understanding this chart helps you figure out where your child sits in relation to her peers, on a national basis.

Now that you have begun to relax – after all, it doesn't seem that complicated – be aware that the Ministry of Education is in the process of *rewriting* the entire curriculum. Aargh! This new curriculum will not feature the Essential Skills, and will endeavour to cut down on the

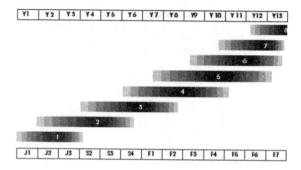

Figure 2

amount of content so that children have the opportunity to use higher-level thinking skills.

This new curriculum will be released to the public in 2005, and is intended to be implemented by 2007.

LEARNING TO READ

One of parents' primary concerns when their child starts school is reading. Parents want and need to know that their child can read, as success in education depends upon it.

When it comes to reading, a child's abilities are assessed in a number of ways. Recognising the letters of the alphabet is important, as is knowing the sounds that the letters make. A child who knows that the letter 'b' makes the sound 'buh' can use this in sounding out words. This is called phonetic awareness.

The teacher will also look at your child's reading behaviours. At a very basic level, they want to know if she knows which way to hold the book, can turn pages and can understand that the print (the words) are conveying a message to the reader. The child who mimics reading understands all these things. The first 'readers' given to children at school help develop this skill.

The teacher will look at the way your child approaches words that she doesn't know – they want to help her gain a variety of approaches to tackle new words. Examples include sounding the word out, breaking the word up into parts, looking for parts that she may already know, and checking whether her word choice makes sense in the context of the sentence that she is reading. Teachers will also be looking at her attitude to reading.

Most assessments about your child's reading ability will come from something called 'Running Records'. You probably remember doing them as a child. This is when a child reads a book to the teacher and he or she marks ticks for correct words. The teacher notes which words were read incorrectly as well as those that the child read wrong and then went back and self-corrected. Following the reading there is usually a set of questions that the teacher asks her, in order to gauge her understanding of what she has read. These tests are done more regularly in the early years of schooling and give your child a 'reading age'.

Some schools give this information to parents, while others do not. I recommend that you make it your business to know how your child is reading. You do not want to wait until your child is nine, only to learn that her reading level is years below her chronological age. If you know, then you can do something about it.

NCEA

The National Certificate of Education Achievement (NCEA) has become New Zealand's method of allocating qualifications. NCEA Level 1 replaces School Certificate, NCEA Level 2 replaces Sixth Form Certificate, and NCEA Level 3 replaces University Entrance (Bursary) exams.

It can be difficult to get your head around NCEA, as it is quite different from our exams of the past.

NCEA Level One:

Awarded to students with a total of 80 Level One credits. Eight of these must be literacy skills (in English and/or Maori) and eight must be numeracy skills.

NCEA Level Two:

Awarded to students who gain 60 credits at Level Two or above, as well as another 20 from any other level – some Level One credits can be used for Level Two NCEA.

NCEA Level Three:

Awarded to students who gain 80 credits, 60 of which must be at Level Three or above. In order to get University Entrance, the student will need 42 credits at Level Three, 28 of which come from an approved list. The student will also need Level Two literacy credits and Level One numeracy credits.

NCEA Level Four (Scholarship):

Level Four NCEA was introduced in 2004 in an effort to acknowledge and challenge the top scholars of the country. While completing their Level Three work, students can opt into Level Four, which involves higher-level thinking skills. It is awarded to students who gain a total of 72 credits at Level Four. Each subject area contributes 24 credits.

Students can study Level Four in one or more subject areas, and will be awarded Scholarship or Outstanding Performance. Students who achieve scholarship in three subjects within three years are awarded a New Zealand Scholarship Certificate.

Getting to know NCEA

Here are some important points to know in order to understand NCEA:

* NCEA has two different standards – Achievement Standards and Unit Standards. A student completing NCEA Level One may be studying English in a course that is labelled *Achievement* Standard or *Unit* Standard. Achievement standards are generally those subjects that were traditionally in the School Certificate and Bursary exams
* when it comes to Unit Standards, individual schools may offer any subjects they choose, such as childcare, first aid or engineering
* students are given a Record of Learning that shows in more detail than previous certificates their areas of strength and weakness

* it uses a credit system, where different types of work are awarded a given number of credits. When you have enough credits, you achieve NCEA

* in each particular subject area there are standards that are worth a particular number of credits. In English, for example, a standard may be the ability to produce formal writing. For each standard, the student will be awarded one of four results: not achieved, achieved, merit or excellence. An overall average will be given in each subject area

* a student can combine Level One, Two and Three courses in a single year

* an NCEA certificate shows that you have completed the required credits, while the Record of Learning shows the areas studied and how well you have done.

Although New Zealand curriculum documents are being rewritten, NZQA and NCEA will remain, so if you can get your head around it, it's well worth understanding.

Know the School

One of the best ways to know what is going on in a school is to be involved, particularly in the Board of Trustees. If you can't be on the board, it is a good idea to know someone who is. There are many things that go on within a school that a parent can only know about through involvement and personal connections.

Checking the school's profile through the Education Review Office (ERO) will give you some idea of the strengths and weaknesses of the school your child attends. ERO reports are available by asking the school or on the Internet.

Individual schools will also have their own philosophies that they adhere to. This will give you insight into what they view as important and their approach to teaching and learning. As a parent, your ideal is to send your child to a school that is compatible with their individual nature. There is no one-size-fits-all school, and it may mean that you send different children to different schools.

Know the Adults Involved in Your Child's Education

The most important adult in relation to your child's education is obviously their teacher. Establishing a positive, open relationship with the teacher will have many positive spin-offs. You are more likely to learn about how your child is doing through an informal chat than from report cards or even parent–teacher interviews. Making an effort to pick your child up from their classroom (even if it is once a month) lets the teacher know you are interested and available to help in the education of your child. You can also give the teacher information about what is going on at home – particularly when it is likely to be affecting their learning, such as a marriage separation.

Code EIGHT

THE OLD CODE: Entertainment

From the youngest age, our children are encouraged to sit back and be entertained. Whether it is in the form of a flashing musical keyboard, or sitting at a PlayStation, children are not creating their environment and experiences, but are encouraged to be receptive participants of their world.

No discussion of entertaining children would be complete without mention of the technologies that have infiltrated our homes. I believe that as parents we need to be *balanced* in our approach to these forms of entertainment. Raging debates about these technologies go through stages – another new study comes out that says how bad these things are for our children, everyone jumps up and down in agreement for a week or two, and then it all settles down. Television stations continue to play violent programmes and more games continue to come onto the market. So, given that's the reality of our modern world, let's try and get some perspective on technology.

The Bad Side of Technology

* Technology violence helps children learn new acts of aggression.
* Technology violence helps make it okay for children to copy what they see.
* Technology violence enables children to participate in the violent experiences of another person.
* Technology violence reinforces the view that the world is a bad place.
* Technology rarely offers creative freedom – the ability to explore ideas and to develop imagination.
* Technology means that children receive immediate gratification and will find it harder to put effort into other types of entertainment that require time and perseverance. It is also linked to ADHD.
* Technology means that your child is sitting still rather than actively playing, therefore depleting his health and contributing to obesity.
* Technology substitutes active experience for passive.

The Good Side of Technology

* Just as children will model violent behaviour, so too will they model good behaviour.
* Children can learn from technology in a way that is self-directed and appeals to their visual and auditory senses. Such learning provides individual instruction that is unavailable in a classroom where there is one teacher to every 20 or 30 students.
* Television, videos, computers and DVDs can provide access to worlds and people beyond the child's immediate environment. For example, children can communicate with people in the Antarctica – asking questions and viewing pictures.

* Technology has enabled students, particularly in secondary schools, to access distance learning with a live teacher.
* Computers provide another means of self-expression and a way of presenting material.
* We live in a technological world, and knowledge of computers is a necessity in the workforce.

As you can see, as much as there are bad aspects of technology, so too are there positive ones.

We need to maintain an active interest in what our children are watching or playing. Obviously, if your child spends hours watching violence or, as PlayStations encourage, participating in violence, there are going to be negative consequences. This isn't hard to work out. Neither is it hard to see that if a child spends hours on his butt in front of a screen, his capacity for imagining is being depleted and he is more likely to get fat.

I believe it is all about balance and choice: providing a limited opportunity for sitting in front of a screen and parent-controlled watching. I'm quite firm about what my children are allowed to watch, and random acts of senseless violence are not a part of my home. Because my children do not depend on television or computers for entertainment, they are forced to use their imaginations to create experiences for themselves. I have spoken to teachers who say that they have noticed in the past decade a massive shift in even the youngest children who lack the ability to play. What they do is *copy* what they have viewed. This is not helping imagination and creativity.

This has sometimes left Kalym feeling isolated because he doesn't know the computer programmes that are being mimicked by his classmates.

Active Brains

And what of creativity? This seems to take a back seat to intelligence when parents are busy and under stress, unless a child is involved in a formalised programme, such as dance or music lessons. Then it matters more because there are exams to sit and competition with other children. But these programmes focus on intelligence rather than creativity – musical or bodily intelligence rather than true creativity.

Creativity is often thought of as mystical, and hard to define and recognise. We look at artists, interior designers, fashion designers, photographers and such like, and we label these people creative. But what of the mum trying to convince her toddler that broccoli is yummy by giving it personalised characteristics and telling a story to get it in his mouth? What of the dad who builds a fort in the backyard for his kids? This is creativity too. Nothing mystical about these acts!

So while being entertained is nice on occasion, let's get rid of this old code and encourage our children towards the new code: creativity.

THE NEW CODE: Creativity

Creative and intelligent individuals are rich in personality traits that can leave parents exasperated or brimming with a mixture of admiration and fascination.

There have been many investigations into the personality traits of creative individuals. Davis and Rimm (1994) did one such study, and they compiled a list of the common traits. (They make the point that not every creative person has every one of these traits.)

Traits of the Creative Personality:

* ✳ confidence
* ✳ risk-taking
* ✳ high energy
* ✳ adventurousness
* ✳ curiosity
* ✳ humour
* ✳ playfulness
* ✳ idealism
* ✳ reflectiveness
* ✳ enjoy spending time alone
* ✳ enjoy activities that are novel, complex and mysterious
* ✳ perceptive
* ✳ intuitive.

If you were beginning to think a creative personality is all good, they do list a few more traits that are likely to make these children harder for parents and teachers to deal with:

* ✳ stubborness
* ✳ uncooperativeness
* ✳ resistance to domination
* ✳ questioning of laws and authority
* ✳ cynicism
* ✳ capriciousness
* ✳ egocentricity
* ✳ tendancy to be withdrawn
* ✳ sloppy
* ✳ forgetfulness
* ✳ indifference to conventions and courtesies.

While the above focuses on creative personality traits, many of these traits can also be applied to the personalities of intelligent individuals.

From these, we can see that ultimately these children are *independent* thinkers. Because they ask questions and are self-reliant, they will often be non-conformers. Having an independent child can be wildly frustrating but, in the end, it will be of benefit to them when they venture out into the world on their own.

What Can a Parent Do?

Creative, intelligent children can be hard work. Don't doubt it for a second.

One of my friends has a son who exhibits almost all of the traits listed above. He overtly expresses his individuality, particularly with clothing. His latest choice of expression is to dress as a punk, so he enjoys wearing a leather jacket, studded wrist and neckbands, and hanging chains around his shoulder. Recently he had a school dance to attend and was very excited to learn that his nanny had been a punk rocker in her day. They spent ages together putting his hair in a mohawk and colouring it red and gold. He went to the dance thrilled with how he looked. When he returned home, he slept carefully so he could keep the style for the following day. Imagine how my friend felt when the following day she did the grocery shopping with him.

On another occasion, he was having bad dreams and came into her bed during the night. She lay there cuddling him, dozing into sleep. Suddenly she got a nudge: 'Mum,' said the boy. 'How old do you have to be to get pierced?' This child is just seven! Hoping to put the desire from his mind, she told him that he had to be much older and that getting pierced hurts. 'It doesn't matter, Mum,' he replied. 'I'll get a general anaesthetic.'

We all have a creative, independent dimension, and perhaps it is easier for the independent parent to support their independent child than the parent who is strict about the 'right' way of doing things.

Our objective as a parent is to acknowledge, support and nurture the nature of our children. How on earth do we do this?

Keep a sense of humour

We must be able to lighten up and appreciate the independent expression of our children in whatever form it may take. If we get hung up on what is deemed appropriate by society we will be trapped by these norms, using them to define our children. In doing so, we will not be able to look past these norms to enjoy the life that our children bring to our world. My friend in the previous example may well have experienced strange looks, and even tut-tuts from observers, but she held her head high and laughed when she shared the story.

Provide emotional support

In many school environments there is not too much scope for a child to express his independence, and as he gets older, he will desire, indeed *require* independent self-expression.

If this is stifled at home as well as at school the result can be a magnification of the negative traits of creativity outlined above. In seeking self-definition, teens can become highly creative and a parent who allows this expression is providing a solid and secure foundation for adult life. If, however, the teen is not allowed to express his individuality, he will find other means of doing so which are more likely to be harmful.

What we need to do is help children find some sort of acceptable balance. Consider, for example, the teen who appears at the breakfast table, ready to go to school – with green hair. You can yell and scream and make him go and wash it out, or you can put it into perspective. Does green hair actually matter? The answer will depend upon the school – is it against the rules? If it is, then you could negotiate with the teen. Yes, you are okay with his green hair, but school isn't. You may discuss why they have this rule and whether you or your teen thinks it is a good rule. If he decides that it is not, then you can talk about whether or not it is worth following this rule. Is it so important to him that he is willing to get into trouble for it? Your job as a parent is to help him adapt to the system, and ultimately, to help him move beyond it.

If you have a highly creative individual, however, look around for a school that doesn't have school uniforms and is more relaxed about personal appearance. If your child is staying at a school with a uniform, let him know that he can wear what he wants after school and during the weekend. You will be less likely to experience rebellion if you have acknowledged his individualism and given him a chance to express it.

Let them create their own environment

Consider your child's bedroom or part of the bedroom, if she is sharing. This is something that you really don't have to be in control of. You may have a particular style when you decorate your home but have you given her a chance to experiment and find her own style? Is she able to express her personality in her own space? If you choose what goes on the walls, what the colour scheme will be and where everything belongs, how will she ever know what she likes? If she paints her bedroom black and dyes her duvet red, she is merely expressing where she is at. Rather than fight it, *listen* to it.

Creativity and intelligence requires space and time. In order to thrive, children need a personal space for their constructions, their art, their music, their writing. In this space, disorder may reign. This is normal! A particular idea may take weeks or even months of work, and if she is required to pack up and tidy every evening it makes it laborious to start again the following day. If she needs a degree of disorder to create, give it to her.

Independence thrives in turbulent passions and a child or young person cannot fully delve into her passions if she is always concerned about keeping everything ordered. From disorder will come order. A palette of mashed paints becomes a work of art.

Back off!

Let your child or teen play.

If she has to justify her creative expressions or intellectual investigations every step of the way, she may either dig her heels in or conform to your expectations. When she chooses to do her hair or decorate her room in a certain way, she is involved in a *process*. She is involved in exploring ideas and beliefs, and if you stop the creative process early on, you are preventing the process from growing to fruition.

Creative thinking involves consideration of any and all ideas. If you block every avenue for the safe expression of independence, such as hair, clothing, art, or music, then she may search for another outlet that may not be safe, such as drugs, destructive eating habits or tagging.

Make it acceptable – even encouraged – to spend time alone, to follow passions and be an individual. The child who is allowed room to question and create is going to be more discerning when it comes to making choices with peers. If she has had rules forced on her without understanding, then she will be a follower, and we all know the risks involved in that.

Ultimately, in order to nurture your child's creative and individual personality, all you need to do is provide her with the freedom to be her own person. Let her think; let her feel; let her do. This is not a free pass to allow irresponsibility without boundaries on behaviour. It is an opportunity to support her individuality and her expression of it, free from judgements, expectations, pressure and surveillance.

Artistic and Aesthetic Interests

Developing creativity in children requires an interest and appreciation of the arts and aesthetics. Some children appear to have more natural talent when it comes to the arts, while others seem to have an eye for creating environments that are aesthetically pleasing. The ability to discern quality is an important skill to learn and is one that *all* children are able to develop regardless of their natural abilities in the arts.

An interest in, and appreciation of the arts is central to understanding not only the society in which we live, but also societies around the world, and ultimately it gives the children an understanding of themselves.

173

The arts are a part of being human – no other species is known to be able to observe, interpret and express experiences or feelings as we do.

In developing artistic *appreciation* in our children we provide them with the opportunity to understand intuitively and empathetically the emotions, beliefs, values and messages that the artist attempts to convey.

In developing artistic *talent* in our children we provide them with a safe means of self-expression – creativity in its highest form.

The arts is a loose term which refers to a wide spectrum of activities encompassing music, visual art, drama or dance. Each of these categories can be further broken down into many different areas. Music, for example, may be composition; knowledge and skills of a particular instrument; enjoyment of a certain type of music, such as the blues; an understanding of rhythm; technical knowledge of musical theory; or singing. The list could go on and on, as the term music incorporates so many different facets. The same applies to each of the four arts.

What Can a Parent Do?

Initiating and maintaining an interest in the arts and aesthetics can be achieved only by exposing your child to the arts. If a child has had no opportunity to view and reflect upon art then they will not have the opportunity to develop artistic taste. Exploration of the arts becomes a way of life for a family, something that is natural and shared. Brought up in such an environment, children will learn through osmosis. Technical knowledge and individual talent may be developed, but this is something else. Here, our focus is on *interest* in the arts. From this interest will grow the motivation for developing artistic talent.

Exposing children to experiences

The first thing you can do is expose your child to as wide a variety of the arts as time, finances and opportunity allows.

Make use of your local community

All communities have some form of art. Local galleries, exhibitions, dance, drama and music performances are an excellent way of exposing your child to a wide range of arts. Check in local newspapers and join the art societies to keep in touch with what is going on in the community. Also, become familiar with the more permanent art structures – the sculptures, murals and buildings that are in your town or city.

Use the library

There are some fabulous books available about the great artists through history. Some are presented as a story for younger children, while others go into greater detail and facts for the older children. Make the issuing of these kinds of books as natural as any other more popular books. Children's books such as these are excellent for learning about a particular artist and their style of art. A book about Van Gogh, for example, will enable the child to learn about his particular style and be able to identify his art when they come across it in other environments. Other useful books are those which are not about a particular artist, but include illustrations which are in themselves works of art, such as the books of Eric Carle.

Listen to a range of music

In the car and at home, music can be played in the background. Classical music is remarkably cheap to purchase and just as a child can come to identify a particular visual artist, so too will they come to learn different composers and their work. They will develop an ear for music, and in time will become discerning about quality and feelings portrayed in music.

Explore your country

If you live in a small town, make it your business to know what art activities are occurring around the country. Some will be close enough to make a day's excursion to a nearby town to view an art performance or exhibition. If you are going on holiday, take the time to map out the galleries and museums along the way and to stop and view them. You may be lucky enough to be in a town on the day where there is a dramatic or musical performance.

Use technology

While I do not advocate children watching hours of television or spending a long period of time at the computer, you can be discerning in what you allow your children to view. Technology is a valid form of artistic expression, and your child will reach a stage where they make choices that reflect quality. For example, there is a wonderful video of Eric Carle's *The Very Hungry Caterpillar*, which includes several other stories as well. The last story on the tape is called *I See a Song*. This is an awesome visual interpretation of music that the author achieves without using a single word. Compare this to the videos that claim to stimulate artistic genius in your child, such as those produced by the Baby Einstein company. These are a tragic misuse of humanity's geniuses. The *Baby Mozart* video, for example, plays Mozart's compositions while displaying a series of plastic toys for the child to view. If I were Mozart, I'd be turning in my grave.

TV listings can let you know about programmes that are coming up that can be valuable learning experiences for your child: artist biographies, performances and quality drama.

Many international art galleries exhibit their work online. Children can view the work without having to actually go to the country where the work is held.

Encouraging children to get involved

Provide as many opportunities for your child to engage in the arts, to become *actively* involved in creating their own artistic expressions.

Create an art space

Have an area of your home specifically set aside for the creation of art. This is an area where a mess can be made, but also where the child learns to care for their art supplies. Have a large table on suitable flooring with shelving for supplies. On the walls display the child's art, as well as the visual art of other people. This needn't be expensive – I have bought old calendars for $2 showing the works of artists such as Michelangelo, and cut them out and presented them as a series of art pieces.

Art supplies can be expensive, particularly those of quality. From my experience, I would far rather pay more for good crayons, pens and paints than the cheaper stuff, which often does not work very well and does nothing for developing taste. However, many things around the home can be recycled for creative pursuits.

What you include for your child to work with in their art space will depend upon the age of the child and their own interests, but some ideas are listed below.

IDEAS OF THINGS TO PUT IN ART SPACE:

* paint
* crayons
* coloured pens
* coloured pencils
* charcoal
* all sorts of paper – coloured, thick, thin, old Christmas and birthday wrapping paper, cardboard, all in a variety of sizes
* glue
* scissors
* materials for collage – glitter, sequins, feathers, leaves, ice-block sticks, buttons, magazines, wool and a variety of scrap material
* food boxes, toilet rolls and milk containers.

Your art space could include a variety of craft and art books, which your child can look through for inspiration. You will find a ton of ideas and suggestions on the Internet, which you can print out and put in a clear file for your child to refer to.

Make music available to everyone

Have a range of CDs and cassettes that your child can put on and listen to. Stereos are not complex for children, and with simple instruction even young children can learn how to look after CDs and stereos. If you cannot stand some of the music your child chooses, or you find that you require quiet when they need noise, have a pair of headphones that they can use.

I also believe that every home needs a microphone. I mean a proper microphone, not a piece of plastic junk. They are so much fun and they give the opportunity for performance and experimentation in a non-threatening manner. If you're the type of person who sings into a hairbrush, why not indulge yourself and your children by playing around with your voice? If they see you doing it, they are likely to try it themselves.

Percussion instruments are the first instruments that a child will be able to use. Because they are designed for rhythm, there is less skill involved in playing them than instruments that require specialised instruction. Rhythm is something that is learned from a very early age and provides a way of knowing music. It begins as intuition – a matter of feeling the beat – which will provide the foundation for under-standing timing, an important skill in recreating a piece of music.

A word about quality. Percussion instruments are available from most toy shops. In most cases they are plastic and sound *awful*. They do nothing for teaching your child about quality in sound. They look tacky and they sound tacky – *stay away from them!* This also applies to cheap recorders and xylophones. If they do not have sound quality they become something that your child will bang around on occasionally, because they will have very little connection with the music that they listen to. No matter how hard they try, they will not be able to get a nice sound.

Good quality instruments can be bought from specialist music shops. Some toy shops may have quality instruments, but in my experience they are few and far between. Another cheaper option is to purchase percussion instruments from the Trade Aid shops that are scattered up and down the country. These shops offer traditional instruments used in countries throughout the world and have good sound quality.

Choosing whether or not your child should take up music lessons will depend upon a variety of factors, such as the interests of the child, the availability of instruments and tutors, as well as parental influence. I know of many an adult who themselves suffered through years of lessons and who refuses to go near the instrument that they were forced to play.

Then there are people like my husband who had only one lesson as a child yet can play piano and guitar by ear very well. I am as jealous as hell because I spent a decade learning classical guitar and still can't play by ear. His playing sounds better, and more people want to sit around and sing with him. However, I do advocate music lessons. I believe there are many benefits of learning an instrument – it is another language for the child to express themselves in as well as to understand others; it is a tangible form of discipline because the child can hear that their practice is paying off; it develops coordination; it brings together the left and right hemispheres of the brain; and with the right teacher and home atmosphere, it is an enjoyable pastime.

Another option is for your child to join a choir or to take singing lessons. Whether or not you formalise their singing in this way, sing often in your home. Children don't care whether you have a good voice or not. (Okay, that may be a bit of a lie – there have been occasions when one of my children has shoved their hand over my mouth and told me to be quiet.) Sing loudly, sing quietly, sing on your own and sing as a family. It is a great form of bonding and can change a mood very quickly. Make up songs; change the words of familiar songs or nursery rhymes. Play with your voice and all the different sounds it can make.

Dance

We cannot really separate dance from music, as the two are inter-connected. Dance, however, is more to do with the body – a physical expression of sound, thought and feeling.

Children love to dance. While some may be shyer about letting go of their inhibitions and dancing, others are quite confident about putting the stereo on and letting their body go. It is an excellent means of using up excess energy, particularly for younger children or children who find it difficult to sit still.

> *My children have grown up dancing. When they were little we used to dance in that horrible 'nightmare' part of the day – you know, when everyone is tired and scratchy and waiting for dinner. It used to work wonders. Now that my eldest is a teen she's more private, but in the evenings her stereo goes on and I can hear her dancing about. I think it's great.*
>
> *Melanie*

You will need to decide if you want your child to take dancing lessons. There are a number of dancing styles around, and if you're the parent of a boy it is becoming a much more acceptable activity for them to engage in. Dancing lessons are excellent for learning body control, developing fitness and flexibility and, of course, they provide another means for self-expression.

Sixteen-year-old Hannah Maclean is rated in the top 20 for her age group in New Zealand for dance, and she firmly believes that dancing provides her with a creative outlet that keeps her on track. When you talk with her she seems just like most other teens, with concerns about friendships and the future – but her dancing makes her that little bit different. It shows her independence and self-motivation and it gives her an opportunity for self-expression and success.

> *I've been dancing for years and I love it. It keeps me busy – I practise around three times a week and last year I started to teach younger kids. It means that I look after myself, and make choices that some other people just don't understand. But that's okay.*
>
> *Hannah*

Have a dramatic life

Married to a drama teacher, I cannot imagine life without dramatics. Drama is an inherent part of our life and it certainly makes things interesting. All of our children are little performers, but even more interesting is observing the children and adults who come into our home. It appears that the environment makes it okay for other people to play – to explore and express themselves in a way they wouldn't do normally.

Drama encourages children to push themselves emotionally and physically in a unique and valuable way. Indeed, I believe that it is one of the most important skills for children to learn. Our society is based on a foundation of oral communication. Drama enables us to express but also to understand other people. In role-playing, for example, we adopt whatever attributes are held by the character whose role we take on. Surely this provides us with the quality of empathy that will ultimately make us more sensitive to other people's needs.

Drama has wider implications. The young person who has learned to take on the role of different people is able to use these skills in the workforce. Consider going for an interview, for example. Even though she may feel scared inside, she can portray confidence and calmness that will help her communicate effectively in the interview.

Drama in the home is about having fun and keeping a sense of humour about life. There are many ways in which children explore the dramatic. In our home, it is not uncommon to have Superman putting out fires in the garden, or a Scottish marching band traipsing through the halls. Our goal as parents is to encourage the children's dramatic creative expressions, even though they drive me barmy on occasion.

Some ideas include:

* **Dress-ups:** A collection of capes, hats and clothing in the home is excellent for children to put on and become a variety of characters. I believe that most dress-up costumes that are available in toy stores are a waste of money because they are generally one thing, so that when the child puts on a ladybird costume, for example, all she can be is a ladybird. Having a variety of materials, hats, shoes and bags make for

much more variety and creativity. These are not expensive things to buy – check out the local op shop or go through your own wardrobe to see what can be passed on. Children can make their own crowns or wands or other items they may wish.

✳ **Room to move:** Dramatic children do not enjoy being confined to small spaces or to one particular area. They like to play in the bathroom, in the kitchen or in their bedrooms. They like to tip couches on their sides and drape large sheets over the top to create houses, caves and magical places. They like lots of cushions. They like to take things from the kitchen to use in the pretend kitchen they have made in the lounge. They can be taught to pick up after themselves, but if you really can't stand the idea of a chaotic home on a particular day, send them outdoors. Mats become magic carpets to take them to faraway lands; chairs get put in a row to become buses or rockets.

✳ **Puppets:** Hand puppets are a quieter option. Although they do not use the full body, they still give children the chance to explore different characters and dimensions of themselves. Make a simple puppet theatre by nailing four pieces of wood in a square, and putting a stand on the bottom. Cut a piece of material in half and sew along the top for a curtain. In their art space, children can make their own puppets and accessories.

✳ **Story-telling:** This is a valuable art as it provides a strong foundation for reading and writing long before these skills are learned. Story-telling is a whole-body experience, where senses are stimulated and there is interaction between the person telling the story and the person listening to the story. Parents have many stories to be told, and children are keen to hear them. If you feel inadequate, begin with stories about your own history or about your child when they were small. As you gain confidence, use your children to direct the story. Begin the story with 'Once upon a time there was a . . .' and allow your child to finish the sentence. Then move on. 'The . . . was having a bad day because . . .' and again allow your child to fill in the blanks. On other occasions, listen to children tell you their own stories. If they find it difficult to go beyond a sentence or two, ask them open-ended questions (ones they can't answer with a yes or no) to get them thinking.

* **Use technology:** Have blank tapes available for them to record their own stories on. This will include using sound effects and different voices. As they get older, let them use a video camera to make their own productions. Most young people love to watch themselves on television. They can make music videos or short films.

* **Toys:** Have a variety of toys that they can use for dramatic play. This includes such things as dolls, stuffed animals, cardboard boxes, appropriate-sized household materials, cars, plastic animals, LEGO® and other miniature items such as a castle with miniature people.

The possibilities for drama in the home are limited only by imagination. Even a meal can become a dramatic adventure by putting down a blanket, calling it a boat and having everyone cram on it for the duration of the meal. Better watch out for sharks!

Like the other arts, there is the option of signing your child up for drama lessons. The success of such an undertaking will very much depend upon the quality of the teacher and their philosophy. Some will be much too focused on working towards a performance for parents at the end of the year and will provide little teaching in the art of drama.

Keep an eye on the local newspaper as community theatre is alive and well in New Zealand and can provide an opportunity for performance.

Encouraging children to form opinions

An appreciation of, and interest in the arts and aesthetics requires an attitude of evaluation – being able to form opinions both about your own work and the work of others. Without personal reflection, exposing and engaging your children in the arts will not enable them to move to the next level of understanding and appreciation. Every experience of art is a process, whether it is one's own work or that of someone else. There are no right or wrong answers in evaluating and reflecting upon art. Encourage your child to go with their gut, to say what comes to mind rather than trying to give 'correct' responses.

It begins simply with a description. You can discuss with your child what happened in the performance or what was in a painting or different works of art within an exhibition. This is not a test of how much they can remember, just an opportunity to recount the experience. Don't be surprised if the things your child noticed were very different from the things that were most noticeable to you.

Next, explore the feelings that were evoked by the art, for what is art without emotion? You may discuss what you think the artist was feeling when they painted a particular piece, as well as what your child felt when they were looking at or watching it. If it is their own piece of art, explore what they were feeling when they created it.

Third, consider why the piece of art was created. Was it just for fun, was there a message that the artist was trying to give, or were they trying to make the audience feel a certain way? If it were the child's own art, what were they trying to do – express a feeling, share an idea, or just play with their creativity?

Next, ask your child his opinion about the art. Did he like it? Why or why not? A younger child may not have the vocabulary to express what he intuitively knows, so don't press him. Now is the opportunity for children to learn the specialised elements and principles of the individual arts.

Finally, decide with your child if he wants to explore it further. If it was a performance, does he want to learn more about it? Is he interested in doing something similar himself? If it was a work of art, he may be interested in learning more about the artist and his or her techniques. He may like to try art in the same style. Alternatively, if it is his own piece of art, get him to consider what he would do differently next time and decide if he would like to do another piece. The story he created on tape, for example, may have been muffled or confused in places. Is he interested in doing another?

Evaluating and reflecting upon art is an important step, but it is not necessary to do this for all your child's art. It will kill his motivation if he has to go through this process each time he draws a picture. It is, however, an important technique to learn and it is worthwhile doing this from time to time. You're the parent: you decide if you think it is appropriate.

One idea is for your child to have a journal of the arts that he uses to glue tickets, write about, or draw or paint responses to what he has seen. Such a journal would also be an excellent reminder of exhibitions and performances your child has been to.

Code NINE

THE OLD CODE: Conformity

We know the importance of a solid education and success, particularly in the high-school years. But how important is it – really? How many of us use what we learned in high school?

Often the basis of our useful, life-long learning has come through our experiences and interactions with other people. Our own motivation and feelings about ourselves, as well as how we want our life to pan out, also plays an important part.

The final years of schooling provide the platform from which our young people can choose their career.

Tertiary education is now big business. The number of private institutions offering qualifications is increasing. The cost of attending these institutions can run into tens of thousands of dollars. The alternative is government-funded tertiary institutions. Government-funded is a far cry from free and these institutions are fiercely competitive. They want your money, and if you don't have it you can always borrow from the government and pay it back once you are working – with an interest rate significantly above inflation. Even the government wants to make a profit from your child's learning. So our young people are put under pressure to get a qualification in order to get a job. It appears that the days of working in order to learn are gone and we must now learn in order to work.

Welcome to the world of fear, confusion and inequality.

> *I just don't want my girls to go to university. My husband and I cannot afford to send them and I would hate for them to have to spend four years at university and come out thousands of dollars in debt. I was paid to do my training – it wasn't much but it meant that we were actually encouraged to get qualified. If I had to do it now, I'd be so far behind financially. Why would I want my girls to carry that kind of debt on their shoulders?*
>
> *Kelly*

> *I don't know what to do if I don't do well in my exams. Mum and Dad keep telling me to just do my best but it's got to be more than that, you know? I want to get a scholarship so that they don't have to spend so much money on me. I'm going to university. I want to be a vet.*
>
> *Alison (17)*

The focus today is very much one-track, with a single message: conform, conform, conform.

Conform to what? To get an education, to start down the adult path thousands of dollars in debt?

Let's take the example of two friends, Angela and Martin, both of whom finish Year 13 with NCEA Level 3. They both gain passes without attaining a scholarship. Both want to be teachers but have parents who cannot afford to send them to university.

Martin decides to go on the dole. He continues to live at home, being paid under the table on occasion, and spends his time surfing in the summer and snowboarding in the winter.

When he turns 25, the government says that he is now independent and funds him through his teacher training. He marries at 26 and has a baby that same year. His wife decides to stay at home with their child. The government increases his student allowance to fund his wife and child.

Meanwhile, Angela goes straight to university following school. She completes a four-year degree and, at 21, ventures into the workforce with around $30,000 of debt under her belt. A couple of years later she falls in love, gets married, has a baby and spends a few years at home with her child.

Let's jump to the future: Angela and Martin are now 30. Martin is teaching and earning around $40,000 per annum while Angela is about to return to work. She now has a child to raise. When she took some years off, her loan continued to increase and she is now $40,000 in debt. While her gross earnings are slightly more than Martin's, they earn around the same amount in the hand because she is paying off her debt.

Martin, having been state-funded for nine years, is free of debt and is in a much better financial position than Angela.

Yes, you will have picked up on the link between Angela and myself.

Is it just me, or is this a *bizarre* message to be sending our young people? If you want to stay at home and do nothing, we will fund you, but if you want a tertiary education and you're under 25, and haven't had a child or chosen to marry, then we will be hands-off – you're on your own! Never mind that you cannot work and study full-time simultaneously. Never mind that you want to contribute to our society. You will pay highly for the privilege – we'll charge you interest and make money from you!

As the system stands, is this the sign of intelligence? Is this why we want our children to conform – so they can have a life like Angela's?

This code of conformity rests on a bed of sand. The truth is, and I am living proof, it is a *lie*.

The people in society who make it work – the doctors, nurses, teachers, midwives, police officers and the like – pay highly for an education that traps them in debt. Increasing housing costs mean that many of the people who serve the community can often not afford to live within it.

Beneath the surface, many parents seem to know that something isn't working but too often the response is to begin activities such as reading and math at an increasingly earlier age. There is no time for play because our children must be the best when they hit five and begin their formal learning career.

This kind of focus on academic achievement would be all very well if the education system hadn't changed from the traditional School Certificate and Bursary exams to NCEA. In order to do well in NCEA, our teens need to be able to think creatively, to make inferences, to have self-motivation. NCEA is not about the memorisation of facts and figures. In essence, NCEA requires both left and right-brain thinking.

So we've got this pressure upon parents for their child to *achieve* and yet there isn't a clear definition of what that actually means. Academic success *is* important – we need to be able to read, to write and to do mathematics. But we also want to be happy, creative, contributing members of society. We are fast becoming a nation that defines success in monetary terms, yet we all know of people who are rich yet miserable.

Personally, I define success as: The fulfilment of potential in creative and intellectual thought and action in an environment that is healthy – physically and emotionally – and where financial needs are met.

Creative and intellectual growth go together. We need both left and right hemispheres of our brain to be developed in order to be functional, happy, healthy adults. Our left brain provides us with the ability to gain specific knowledge, to undertake goal-setting and to think critically. Our right hemisphere helps us intuit what other people are thinking and feeling, gets us in touch with how we are feeling and helps us look at things from a holistic perspective. In other words the right hemisphere of our brain allows us to see the whole picture.

We need to step back and look at the messages we are being sent by people who are clearly desperate for our money and look at the wider picture. When we do this, we can begin to let go of our fears for our children and find a more innovative approach to their education.

THE NEW CODE: Innovation

Mark Treadwell is making waves in education circles. He is helping reshape the education system by smashing the code of conformity and moving towards a code of innovation.

Well aware of the impact of technology on education, Treadwell has worked in a variety of roles around the world, helping teachers, schools and educational systems move away from a curriculum based on the accumulation of knowledge to one that is relevant to modern society. He is an author, speaker and consultant for individual schools, clusters of schools and for the Ministry of Education.

His aim is to move the emphasis in the schooling years away from a just-in-case mentality – that we must fill children's heads with specific knowledge just in case they need to know it one day. A massive paradigm shift is taking place. With our technological and information society, children do not need to know the name of 13 capital cities in 13 countries (anyone who can spell G-O-O-G-L-E can get this information), but they do need to be able to ask questions, to make comparisons – in essence they need to be able to *understand* rather than *know*.

Treadwell is forcing the education system to look at its conformity and ask 'Why'? For example, a major focus in today's education system is on children's writing and reading skills. In reality, however, oral communication skills are far more valuable in our present society. He laughs at how we spend the early years telling our children to sit down, sit still and shut up, and then spend the later years not understanding why they don't want to get up and give a speech.

Our present conformity is based on an historic ideal that has very little to do with what works *today*. His focus is on encouraging schools to become inquiry-oriented – places where children can explore their natural curiosity with the world and learn.

Our children will be confronted with mammoth amounts of information. It is more important for them to be able to make discerning decisions about the information than to memorise facts and figures.

As a father of two, Treadwell does not encourage his children to conform to the system either. University is not the only option – he encourages young people to look for different, and often better, ways of achieving their goals.

As parents, we have a lot to learn from his insights and research. Instead of filling our children's minds with specific knowledge – as many tutors and after-school programmes do – he encourages us to remember that these are not 21st-century skills. While they may help a child pass an exam, they will not help her find success in life.

What we can attempt to do is encourage our children to be *innovative*. We can attempt to develop their thinking skills so that they have the capacity to sit back and make decisions based on observation, experience and research, rather than conforming to a lifestyle just because everyone else is doing it.

Thinking creatively and critically involves asking questions and finding solutions. It includes the ability to wonder, to see things in a different light from that which is directly before us.

Edward de Bono is well known for his explorations into both intelligence and creativity. He believes that lateral-thinking skills can be deliberately developed, whereas insight, creativity and humour are things that we can only hope we were born with. His Six Thinking Hats technique for developing lateral thinking is widely accepted. While interesting, valid and well worth investigating for the interested parent, it is a formalised technique which may leave us feeling very guilty if it doesn't work.

Developing creative and intelligent thinking skills is more a way of life than something that is done between 4.00–5.00 p.m. on a Thursday.

THINKING SKILLS INCLUDE:

* originality
* curiosity, problem finding
* risk-taking
* finding similarities and differences
* imagination, exploration
* taking the known to the unknown and the unknown to the known
* flexibility
* open-mindedness
* sensitivity
* problem solving.

What Can a Parent Do?

Fostering thinking skills in our children can make home life very interesting indeed. It can be as complex or as simple as a parent is able to cope with. Be forewarned though: a thinking child can be harder work because she will not accept it when you fob her off with a 'Because I said so' response to her questioning why her curfew is at midnight while all her friends are allowed to stay out as late as they want.

Get involved in play

I am not talking about sitting down and having a family board-game night. I am not talking about giving your child an 'educational' toy to play with. I'm talking about those moments where you can let go of your own seriousness and hang-ups and just play. The following are games to play when you've got a moment with your child (any age can play). They require nothing except time and a sense of adventure.

* **What if?** Both parent and child ask and answer 'what if' questions. Some examples: what if the dinosaurs still roamed the earth? What if it was daylight 24 hours a day? What if today was the last day of the world? What if the world was all green? What if money didn't exist? You get the idea. Don't come up with them all yourself – you'd be surprised by what even the youngest child can think of.

* **Rhyme time:** Create long poems where the last word of every line rhymes. Alternate between adult and child.

* **Jumping words:** One person says a word, and the other person says the first word that comes to their mind. Without pausing, the original person responds to the new word. Keep going for as long as possible without stopping.

* **Gibberish guff:** Set a time limit, for example, a car trip or meal, and make the only allowable conversation to be in made up gibberish. Explore how tone of voice and body language must be used to understand each other. This can be changed to any number of things, limited only by your imagination, such as silence, American accent only, or everyone being robots.

* **Three things:** One person says, 'Three things that you can sing, three things to do with . . . (Insert anything here – yellow, trees, people, happiness, space – whatever.)' Without thinking, the next person must sing three words to do with the chosen subject matter.

* **What next?** The first person tells part of a made-up story and then asks the next person 'What next?' The second person responds, and when finished asks again 'What next?' It keeps going until the story dies an appropriate death.

* **If I was . . . :** Take turns saying 'If I was . . . (a cat, a piece of broccoli, George W. Bush, the Prime Minister, a parent, a kid – anything you can think of) then I would . . . (eat humans, jump off a bridge, sing as loudly and as often as I liked).'

* **Sky secrets:** Lie beneath the sky and search for pictures or images in the clouds or stars.

* **Inventing the uninvented:** Explore all the things that you would invent that haven't already been invented.

* **Would you rather . . .?:** Take turns asking, 'Would you rather be a . . . (cat, ocean, apple, couch) or a . . . (pea, mountain, hammer, song)?' The other person answers the question with or without explanation.

Have a talking home

Talk to your child – often. Reflect on all aspects of their lives, generally in the role of listener. Know what interests them in school, what struggles they're having and so on. If you are a super busy parent, encourage your child to write to you. I know of a number of parent-child relationships that have flourished with email communication.

Challenge your children about decisions they have made, helping them to think through both the positive and negative consequences. When problems or needs are brought up in the house, work together to try and solve them. Have a 'How can it be done?' attitude.

Encourage your child to ask and then answer questions. If they have a question about the stars or dinosaurs or politics, encourage them to seek answers for themselves, rather than giving them your opinion or knowledge. Visit the library regularly, allow access to the Internet, have reference books at home. Make sure they know how to use these resources. Discuss their answers and ideas with them, encouraging them to reflect on their answers.

> *We were on our way to a weekend at the snow and Reid (five years) was very quiet in the backseat. After a while he asked: 'Dad, how do snails know where they are going?'*
>
> *When we stopped, we went and found some snails and spent ages looking at the way they move and at their eyes.*
>
> *Mark and Sharon*

Ask *them* questions – my Dad is a master at this. When I was a teenager, rather than giving me answers he would ask me questions that required me to go away and think (sometimes for weeks) before returning to him with an answer. Not that I'd be let off the hook then – it was more than likely he'd fire another question at me that turned what I thought I knew upside down, and I'd have to go and explore, think and reflect all over again.

Don't own the knowledge in your house.

Value higher thinking

When you value your child's thinking, she is more likely to value it herself.

When your child approaches you with questions, stories or imaginings, be positive. Encourage her wildest ideas. Value her alternatives, her humour and the way she has fun. Respect her ideas, problems and solutions as you would those of any adult individual. Even if you already know that something will not work, let her try to find this out for herself. Don't limit her with your knowledge, but allow her the opportunity to try things out. If you acknowledge and appreciate her higher thinking, she is more likely to try something new or explore something in greater depth. Try to let go of the idea that there is an answer to everything, or that there is a right way of doing things. This attitude is stifling for the development of both intellectual and creative thinking.

Release your expectations

Parents who are thinkers themselves will find it easier to let go of their expectations and enjoy observing the thinking process their child is going through. Always remember that your view of her endeavours will be filtered through your interpretations of her efforts and even the world. It is important to celebrate her apparent failures, focusing on the process, not the end product.

Encouraging perseverance is also important. Creativity and intelligence is not about trying something, finding it doesn't work and then stopping. While in some cases this may be appropriate, it would be better to ask the child if there are any alternatives to her solution.

Have a sense of humour

A sense of humour is intrinsically linked to creativity and intelligence. We need to be able to laugh at ourselves and at each other. My husband Tony has changed my entire perception of life by making me laugh. I came to him with emotional insecurities and a cynical view of the world and the people in it. Most of these are now healed because he helps me lighten up and see the funny side of things.

Life is so much more enjoyable when you can laugh. Did you know that you can even laugh during labour? The importance of humour in a home cannot, I think, be underestimated.

Humour wipes away fears, dries tears and creates a feeling of adventurousness in life.

Tony has affected all members of my family with humour, and each of us has our own expression of it. We tell jokes, we make up new words to songs and rhymes, and we *play*. I could list so many instances where Tony's humour has held our family together and helped us through troubled times. I love watching him around other people because he loves to find the line and then jump over it, unsettling and challenging the most rigid of people.

When it comes to creativity, humour in the home means that we can all safely explore and try new ideas or activities. As Tony says, 'You're breathing, what else matters?' We can be as nutty as we like, we can create an absolutely appalling piece of art and laugh at it, we can sing off-key as loudly as we want. We can dance to '80s music; we can indulge our wildest dreams and ideas and have moments that are free from judgement.

Humour is a gift to creative and intellectual freedom.

Involve your child

While time to yourself is important, so too is involving your child in your world.

When a parent thinks through things aloud, they are giving their child the opportunity to witness creative and intellectual thought processes that she will, through time, absorb. When confronted with a problem, talk through it using creative-thinking skills. Your highly observant and sponge-like child will grow up naturally using these skills, as to her they will be a normal way of thinking.

Teach your child how to learn

Learning how to learn is worthy of a book in itself. In order to function well in society, your child will need to know how to learn – how to find and gather information, how to sort through it to find that which is most useful and how to apply the information.

Such abilities require an understanding of the learning process. While your child is in the midst of her schooling, however, teachers, via the curriculum documents, will dictate much of what she learns.

ENCOURAGING EFFECTIVE LEARNING

In order to effectively learn, your child needs to understand some basic principles:

The importance of environment

* comfort
* space to spread out

* adequate ventilation
* access to pens, paper and other stationery items
* a noticeboard and/or whiteboard
* background noise such as radio or complete silence, depending on the preferences of the individual child
* Adequate lighting

The importance of physical health

* regular exercise
* lots of fresh fruit and vegetables
* high intake of water
* adequate rest

The importance of goal setting and evaluation

* keep a record of goals and whether they were achieved
* goals help provide motivation
* goals need to be realistic and achievable
* goal setting develops independence, encouraging child to work at their fullest capacity
* evaluation encourages self-reflection

The importance of emotional health

* supportive friends and family
* ability to spend time on own without feeling lonely

The importance of time management and organisation

* have a term overview where your child can jot down when assignments are due
* for each major assignment or test, create a step-by step plan for what is required. Give each step a date for completion
* set aside time each day for learning
* have a flexible weekly schedule so that your child can see what is coming up and prepare. If they have a test on Tuesday, for example, then Monday's learning time should be spent studying for this test.

When these basic elements are met, the stage is set for learning to take place.

Your child will also need to be able to do the following:

Complete assignments

* understand the question or requirements. This may seem obvious, but it is something often overlooked
* gather information
* take notes
* use highlighter pen and other visual cues
* summarise information
* keep notes together
* use personalised shorthand
* interview people
* use the library and Internet
* make use of bold and italic print to find overview of information
* scan information to find what is needed

Organise information

* find the main ideas and highlight these or place them at the top of the page
* sort through remainder of information, linking it with the main idea that it supports. This will be the background information, including examples and explanations

Presenting information

* this will usually be teacher-dictated – speech, essay, report or chart. For this, your child will need to understand the importance of presentation skills – and know how to use them

Study for tests and exams

* take notes
* review notes
* make use of memory aids, such as: mnemonics; mind maps; imaginary flashing lights around important information; or little 'movies' to imprint sequenced events, such as in physics or history

* self-test
* review just before test or exam.

Let your child play

I've mentioned this often enough, but here it comes again because *play is the foundation upon which our intelligence and creativity develops.* If this seems like a far-reaching statement, consider it in a practical sense:

Bobby has a set of blocks that he plays with at age two. Bobby creates (imagines) that these blocks become all sorts of different things – a baby, a car or truck, a bridge, a house and so on. He takes the raw material (blocks) and allows his mind to fill in the gaps until he can 'see' with his mind's eye the things he wishes. As Bobby gets a bit older he begins to devise tools out of these blocks. He finds a piece of thin rope and designs pulleys or levers.

As Bobby gets even older he puts the blocks aside. He then comes across abstract concepts in high school and university that require him to 'see' – in the same way he did as a toddler – the meaning behind given symbols, such as those in the sciences and mathematics.

At four, Michelle listens to fairy tales regularly. They appeal to her with their truths about humanity and their power of language, which allows her to bridge the worlds between animals and humans. Later, she lives out the fairy tales again and again, using concrete objects (stuffed toys, blocks, etc.) and using her imagination to fill in the blanks. Gradually she adds to and changes the stories to help her make better sense of her world.

And then comes the exciting day when Michelle imagines stories but does not require concrete objects to help her 'see' what she wants. She can rely totally upon her own mind and imagination to create the world she wants.

In high school and university, the ability to create within her mind helps her appreciate literature and ultimately enables her to write her own.

You can see that play lays the foundation for future learning. Educational videos do not. Neither does television, flashcards, PlayStations or

CD-Roms. Too much of any of these things prevent neural connections being made, as they are linear and do not require the imaging (imagination) that is a baseline for understanding many of our societal subtleties and abstractions – ultimately post-formal operational development.

Back off!

Closely linked to letting your child play is the importance of learning to back off and let them be.

Give your child – whatever their age – credit for their intelligence.

You do not need to know or be in control of everything that is going on in their mind. This is important for a few reasons. First, it helps your child develop independence in thought and action, something we have already ascertained is important in higher-level thinking. If he is struggling with his homework, don't jump in and help him immediately. Let him struggle and see if he can overcome the difficulties on his own. His intellectual growth cannot take place if you are the constant source of intelligence for him.

Secondly, adults are prone to expect articulation of concepts, actions or behaviours that the child may not understand. Asking a child 'What are you doing?' forces him to give an explanation to keep Mum or Dad happy, rather than being able to let his train of thought continue until it reaches a point where he is happy – where understanding has been gained.

Take, for example, a sports-mad child. If he sits for an hour staring out the window, it may seem that he is being 'lazy' or 'wasting time' but in reality he may be working through a tennis serve again and again in his mind – perfecting it. If stopped, he is pulled from his vision and will probably find it hard to explain verbally what he was doing. Or maybe a child is not doing anything of the sort but merely staring into space, living out a variety of fantasies that may be inappropriate to share with Mum or Dad.

This kind of 'vacant' thinking (often associated with the right hemisphere) is important for intellectual development. It depends upon conscious thought relaxing its hold and allowing more creative, holistic and intelligent solutions or understandings to develop.

Code TEN

THE OLD CODE: Pressure

The old codes of perfection, genius and conformity all merge together like a pressure cooker in every parent's gut. Even when logic should prevail, we still feel the pressure of what our children should be, and we – sometimes inadvertently – place this pressure on our children.

We know we shouldn't pressure our children, don't we? There is such a fine line between being supportive and pressuring them. The balance is difficult to achieve: sometimes we'll get it, and other times we won't.

The fact is, we are shooting ourselves in the foot when we pressure our children. Parental pressure on children reduces their capacity for self-reliance and self-esteem. The parent is essentially taking away the child's ability to set goals and make plans for himself. Most successful people have healthy self-esteems – a child under pressure does not. Those parents who do pressure their children tend to increase this pressure over time.

Control is the issue when it comes to parental pressure. It is an ideal held by the parent for their child. Rather than encouraging autonomy, the child is encouraged to conform to the ideal about them held in the parent's mind. Most children will never meet this ideal. In extreme circumstances, particularly as they reach their teen years, these young people either lash out against their parents and engage in drugs, alcohol, sex, violence or truancy, or they engage in more subtle yet just as devastating behaviours such as destructive eating habits – resulting in anorexia and/or bulimia.

Responding to the desire and pressure to do the right thing by our children, many of us have begun to run our children as we would our own lives, or even our work. It's one thing to be organised but it is quite another to be so goal-orientated that every moment of our children's world has an objective and a timetable for how to get there.

It would be difficult to pinpoint when or why we became so obsessive about child rearing. Perhaps, as I've mentioned earlier, it is because our children are *planned* children. (Okay, mine weren't, but most people I know with kids got pregnant intentionally.) The Baby Boomers were the first generation ever to be able to take a pill to prevent pregnancy until they were ready – hence they often delayed having children, making every child a wanted child.

Maybe, as discussed earlier, it is because we now have so much information regarding child rearing that we have become obsessed. Many parenting books these days include checklists for behaviour; others have them for 'developmental milestones' – so there is a nice schedule for what your child should be doing and when (walking, talking and so on). With Kalym, I knew all about what should be occurring and when. What pride I would feel when he was more 'advanced' than the average child, but then, what a knot of panic – fear almost – when he failed to do what he was meant to do.

By the time I got to Malachy, all books of this sort were long put away. None of it really matters. Of course, a child who is significantly developmentally delayed is concerning, but this will be picked up by the GP or Plunket nurse. So Malachy was left to be who he wanted to be by a much more relaxed mum. Without having to record or analyse everything he did, life was a heck of a lot easier for us both. And guess what? I still think he is amazing and I can still see his uniqueness – but it is based on what he has taught me about himself, rather than what I have endeavoured to teach or encourage him to do.

If we look only to these 'developmental milestones', we fail to see so much of the really interesting stuff that each child carries within.

There is pressure on parents to make every moment an 'educational experience'. The fact is that we are putting *our* objectives onto our children and are preventing them from fully experiencing an activity in their own way. We are blocking them. For example, little Anne is in the backseat of the car, and there's a traffic jam. No point in wasting perfect learning time! Mum starts counting cars out loud because Anne is learning her numbers. Meanwhile, Anne, who was watching how the rain trickled down her window, is forced to stop and listen and learn about numbers.

We are overscheduling and pressuring our children because of our *own* fears. We fear that they won't be successful in life. We fear that they will not find their passion, their gift, their reason for being in the world. We fear that they will be normal. Average. Boring. We fear our own abilities as parents so we must, just *must* produce the next genius in whatever field that may be, but preferably more than one. So, quick, let's sign them up for singing, piano, athletics, reading, maths, art and accelerated learning lessons – the sooner the better, because they've only got one chance to be the best. Is it that we want them to be the best, or do *we* want to be the best?

If we look honestly at ourselves, we can acknowledge that the scheduling of our children's lives is more to do with our own insecurities than how it will benefit them.

We do three things when we timetable our children's world, none of which does anything for creating the next Einstein.

First, we give our children a single message – that they, in and of themselves, are *not enough*. We are teaching them that who they are and the things they do are not good enough, that they must be more, be better. We are telling them that they don't have the skills necessary to be successful in life and that we must be their provider. We are telling them that what they want is secondary to what we have decided they need.

Let's return to Maslow and his hierarchy of needs. After physical needs are met, the second tier of needs involves emotional development – healthy relationships, security, self-respect and self-esteem. Success in life can be predicted more by these factors – combined with motivation – than whether or not Zoë was the sports star of the region when she was five.

Other researchers have shown again and again that the quality of relationships a child has will affect their learning, their thinking and their abilities far more than scheduled moments on a calendar.

More than lessons and education, our children need values, security and love. They need time in our world; they need time when we enter their world. They need hugs and cuddles and stories. They need time to laugh and to watch their parents laugh. They need to work through their own problems, and they need to watch parents work through theirs. They need moments of boredom, they need time when they come second to their parents – like sitting at the dinner table while the adults hold boring conversations.

The second thing we do to our children by overscheduling them is serve to limit them. It is not considered okay to send the kids outside to play for a couple of hours, because they may be wasting precious learning time. But hang on a minute – isn't being chucked outside to create new games or make discoveries or even to stare into space a way of actually *increasing* intelligence and creativity?

Finally, when we over-plan our children's lives we leave them vulnerable to suffering from the same physical and mental illnesses that afflict adults. Young dancers with osteoporosis; athletes with broken bones; bent spines from the weight of bags; depression; ulcers – kids have them all these days. Not something I want for my children.

If we return to the CBS documentary about the 'Echo Boomers', Doctor Mel Levine of the University of North Carolina says of the children: 'They have been heavily programmed . . . [Their] whole lives have really been based on what some adult has told them to do.'

There are consequences for our children, but there are consequences for us, too. When we structure our lives around our children, we give up the opportunity to be adult. We make our world all about their world and miss out on enjoying normal, everyday pleasures.

So let's relax about our lives, let's enjoy it more. Let's dump our schedules and to-do lists. Let's *stop* putting undue pressure on our children. Put the old code of pressure in the bin and stick to the new code: opportunity.

THE NEW CODE: Opportunity

Our aim is not to pressure our children, but to provide them with the opportunity to reach their potential – in the widest sense of the word.

Without resources, support, time and adequate mentoring, our children will not have the opportunity to develop intellectually and creatively.

What Can a Parent Do?

Believe in the capacities of your child

Your belief in your child is necessary for their achievement. Your disappointments are things they will intuitively feel. Your assumptions about them will also be felt, whether or not they understand these assumptions. Believing in the capacities of your child requires honest soul-searching as to what your expectations and assumptions are. If they are too high and your child doesn't meet them then your disappointment will be felt by them. If they are too low, then your child will feel it necessary either to prove themselves to you, or worse, to live up to your lowered expectations.

It is a matter of striking that fine balance between pushing your children outside their comfort zone but not so far out that they will drown. Many children will work at the expected level. If they can get away with not putting in the hard yards, they will.

Nurture your child's uniqueness

Some forms of intelligence and creativity are more obvious than others. As parents we need to find out what it is that makes our children unique – where their strengths lie. Let's keep searching until we find out.

Make intelligence and creativity a way of life

If children grow up in a home where it is normal to ask questions, to be curious, to challenge and be challenged, they absorb this approach to life. It becomes something natural, rather than something that needs to be taught.

Be your child's greatest audience

Whether it is a piece of art, a construction out of blocks, a poem or a conversation, your children will find self-esteem and security if you are there, backing and supporting them. They cannot be spoilt with attention, but they can be spoilt with the wrong sort of attention – such as judgement or criticism. Whatever you place your greatest emphasis on, they will too. If the only way to get attention is to misbehave, this is what they will do. If they can get your positive affection and attention by sharing their thoughts, learning and creations with you, this is what they will focus on.

In school, your children are competing against dozens of others, all vying for their teachers' attention. In your home they are competing against all of the demands that you have, but they still require appreciation, attention and affection.

It is just as important not to be too over the top with your praise and attention with things that your child hasn't put much effort into. When Kalym was five, he used to spend up to an hour and a half creating intricate drawings and colouring them in. When he went to school, he would just scribble. I was in the classroom one day and he rushed up to his teacher with a star that he had scribbled all over. The teacher exclaimed her delight, saying how wonderful it was. He looked at me for the same approval – and did not find it. He laughed at me, knowing exactly what I was thinking, and went back to his table to colour it in using all his capabilities. I am sure, by the way his teacher looked at me, that she thought I was not being supportive or a 'good' mum, but I wasn't about to praise something that was far below his abilities.

Give your child resources

The term resources refers to the library, a computer with Internet access, extra-curricular activities and anything else that your child may need in his intellectual and creative journeys.

All of these things cost money, so choices will have to be made with regards to how much you can offer your child. Don't let your guilt strings be pulled if you cannot provide all that you would like – goodness knows I've spent years not being able to give my children what I think they need or deserve. You may need to use your own imagination and creativity if you do not have access to something that you would like. I am a huge advocate of the Internet, as it offers a vast number of activities and ideas – which can be printed off and used.

Give your child time

If every hour of every day is planned to the last minute, if a child is kept busy with extra-curricular activities every day of the week and weekends are filled with what you deem important, then your child will have no opportunity to explore his own creative and intellectual capacities.

Often, when your child is in the classroom, the teacher has a certain number of activities or objectives that he or she needs to cover on any given day. This means that students who need time for reflection or who are slower at completing their work will sometimes be forced to abandon work in order to move on to the next thing. When at home, your child can be given the opportunity for time that is not rushed, and he can indulge his own interests.

Time spent alone also does wonders for children's emotional security and confidence.

Encourage your child's imagination

The gathering and learning of facts and figures is only one way of developing a child's vivid imagination. Their stories, games and fantasies often fill in the gaps around knowledge. Indeed, the younger a child is, the more real their imaginings are – they can find it hard to differentiate between what is real and what is fantasy.

These imaginings stem from the right hemisphere of the brain and provide the foundation for creativity. As their linear knowledge increases, so too should their capacity for creativity – something that can only be learned when they are given the opportunity.

Your child's imagination provides an exciting world that seeks its own form of expression. How you respond to this will affect whether he feels accepted.

All higher thinking begins in the imagination. Consider the scientist who 'imagines' a cure. From this, he works backwards, applying linear knowledge to attempt to reach a solution. An artist 'imagines' an image before she creates it. A writer 'imagines' a story before he sets about penning it.

If your child needs expert instruction, get it

Just as we would send our budding athlete to tennis lessons, so too can we support the child who is good at mathematics or science. However, in some circumstances, you will be unable to find someone to help your child so then you become the 'expert', the educator.

Encourage independence

Without independence, your child will be constantly seeking your approval and not achieving to his highest potential.

Independence involves having the confidence and willingness to try new things, to create and to make mistakes. If your child is fearful of your responses, he will be hesitant to follow his own path.

One of the biggest forms of disservice we do to our children is to force them to be overly dependent on us. It is a matter of trying to find the balance between pushing them to find their potential without applying undue pressure.

Encourage your child to keep a journal

Life can become a series of disjointed events without the opportunity for reflection. Journal writing (or drawing) gives the opportunity for reflecting upon feelings, events and goals. In essence, a journal helps a child to better understand both himself and the world around him. A journal is a safe means for expressing original thoughts, and other thoughts that may be deemed inappropriate within the education system or even within the family.

To know oneself is of great benefit to everyone but for the child and later the teen it will help them in making career choices, love choices and other life choices.

Code ELEVEN

THE OLD CODE: Minor Men

I used to be a feminist. I used to think that men and women were created equal, and that feminism had improved the life of women forever more. Then, at 21, I got pregnant.

By 22, I was a solo mother on the DPB, suffering from major depression. In 12 short months, I had gone from a confident, capable (and admittedly selfish and narcissistic) woman to a tired, stressed, poor and lonely mother.

I learned that as soon as a woman became pregnant, she did not have an equal footing to men. I learned that a man could choose whether or not he wanted to be involved in his child's life, but a woman just had to get on with it. I learned that a man could choose whether he wanted to financially support his child. I learned that child support is *not* a given and that financial deprivation lies on the shoulder of the mother, while a man's weekly contribution can stand at less than a packet of nappies.

I learned in the years that followed that once a woman does go out to work, she is responsible for the cost of childcare, clothing, medical expenses and food, while the father may or may not continue with his meagre weekly payment of $10.

I learned that being a solo mother means that you are vulnerable as a worker. I learned that solo motherhood without the support of the father means you are more at risk of emotional and physical abuses.

A decade down the track, I still see mothers as being among the most vulnerable members of our society for a multitude of reasons, but we'll get to those in a minute. This is in no way meant to demean those men who are struggling to raise children on their own. Statistically speaking though, they are not as common.

One of my biggest difficulties in the mothering journey has arisen because of a lack of role models. When I look around I just don't see many women with whom I can identify, mainly because the images presented are often extreme.

In modern history, there are two images of woman – neither of which fits my view of myself. The first is our idyllic 1950s and 1960s woman. She doted on children and husband and took great pride in maintaining the perfect home, never admitting to the inner consequences of living a self-sacrificing life. Her question when the children left home was: *Is this all there is?* The second is our 1970s and 1980s woman. With big hair, shoulder pads, career and, most important, *independence*, she took great pride in working in a man's world, climbing up the career ladder and earning an enviable income. Her question, when she reached the top and looked around was also: *Is this all there is?*

Nowadays, each of our historical mums is still alive and well. Each has her own magazines, books and set of friends.

Modern celebrity mums get their fair share of magazine covers and stories. The only problem with this is that, 99 per cent of the time, the mum has a 'miracle' pregnancy or birth, they 'love' and 'adore' their new lifestyle and their baby is always, always 'precious'. Yawn. What they fail to mention, in their glorification of celebrity motherhood (especially solo motherhood), is the lack of financial stress experienced by the celebrity mum, plus the availability of the nutritionists, the cooks, the cleaners, and the nannies to look after babe while Mum rids her body of any evidence of its former, pregnant state. They don't mention the number of women who opt for Caesarean sections four weeks before delivery date so that they can walk away without having their stomach stretched to maximum capacity and can retain their designer vaginas.

These magazines also fail to mention the amount of airbrushing that goes on before their pictures go to print. So, while some celebrity mums (thanks, Linda Clark) have the courage to be honest, most don't. Let's ignore them and start coming to terms with *our* reality.

Our mission, I believe, is to start putting a new face on mothering. We have a lot to learn, from the good women of the 1950s and 1960s, as well as from the strong women of the 1970s and 1980s. As with any massive societal change, things swing on a pendulum. We swung to the right and idealised mothers, trapped them at home and took away their right to a brain. Rebelling against this, the next generation of women swung to the left and fought for their right to have a brain and be rewarded for work with equal pay.

Then, during the 1990s, it appeared that some sort of balance was struck. Women didn't need to be *either* career woman or mother – they could be *both*. Women could have it all.

The self-help, self-satisfied and self-orientated ideal took hold and many of us went along for the ride. Life was about *me*. The common cries were : 'I need to find myself,' 'I need some time just for me,' and 'What about me?'

The 'me' phase of the '90s gave everyone the permission they needed to be as selfish as they pleased. This has also created the trap of the eternal adolescent, who can remain so even after having children.

Now we have arrived at the new millennium, and with it's arrival we must create a new understanding of what it is to be a mum. We need to take the bits we like and dispense with the bits we don't.

I believe that all we need to do is shift our perspective. Instead of having to choose between heart and head, dependence and independence, we need to look at all of these things – with honesty.

Can women have it all? Look around and see if you can identify *any* woman who has it all. I bet you can't find her. So while it may sound as though I am supporting the selfish '90s view that we can have it all, I am not.

It is a matter of taking into consideration all facets of our being, as well as our partner and, most important, our children. Instead of looking at instant gratification and satisfaction, mothering needs to be viewed holistically, with all its implications. We need to look honestly at the long-term consequences of our decisions.

Now it is time to turn the tables on the 1990s – it is not about *me*, it is about *us*.

The feminist revolution – which was exciting and all very good – tried to convince everyone that men and women were equal, and neither needed the other. Guess what? They do!

We need to admit that men are just as important in the family as women – kids *need* their dads. While not all men will live up to their responsibilities, there are many wonderful fathers out there who are raising children side by side with the mothers. Not only that, but there are a number of men who are actively pursuing societal change, whether within the home or the school community, in business or in the political arena.

People often ask me how I cope with four children. The answer is not terribly hard for me to find. I cope because I've got a wonderful man who is my best friend and an active dad. Four children with a good partner are *infinitely* easier than one child on your own.

I remember when Lachy was around two months of age. I was shattered beyond belief. He woke up screaming, and I groaned as a familiar knot gathered in my stomach (I had lived with it until Kalym was around two years of age.) Tony leaned over and asked what was wrong.

'I just don't think I can do it,' I replied.

His response? He said that I didn't have to, got up and looked after

Lachy himself. That moment was life-changing for me. It was then that I realised that I wasn't on my own, and that he was with me for the hard yards.

Men have had their work cut out for them too. While women were once pushed *into* the home, so too were men pushed *out of* the home. Now I think we are coming to a point where we realise that we all have something to offer. Women don't need to act like men and men don't need to act like women. We are who we are.

In my house, as in a lot of houses these days, there's a new set of rules. There are jobs to be done so we just get on with them. Five years down the track, I've got jobs that I do, Tony's got jobs that he does. No big deal. One of his main jobs is doing the meals. I can't stand cooking and he finds it a good way of winding down after work. In the mornings we both work to get out the door. In the evenings we both work to get the kids in bed.

Women need to welcome men back into the home – raising children involves women *and* men and it is no small task for either. But I won't rabbit on further about what it means to be a father in this day and age. Who better to talk about it than a man?

Dear reader, brace yourself – it's time to meet my husband, Tony Gilbert.

THE NEW CODE: Major Men

When my wife asked me to write a chapter for her book on parenthood I thought, 'You must be kidding.' I was convinced that she was writing some kind of parenting manual.

To be honest, I have never read one from start to finish – 'Do this, do that . . .' Fortunately, she made my part simple – she wanted me to answer the question, *How does becoming a father make you more of a man?*

My first reaction was to laugh. I had a vision of a Colin Meads lookalike with a chainsaw in one hand and a packet of Huggies in the other and the slogan underneath: 'Real Men Are Real Dads.' In this vision the son gives his father a drawing of Dad with bulging muscles and what might be mistaken for a faint shaft of light emanating from his backside. The boy says, 'I love you, Dad' and you can *almost* see tears forming in the man's eyes. He slings his son over his shoulder and they go off to feed on a dead animal.

I have a different scenario.

I wake up in the morning to the low-level drone of a whining child. I stare at the usual spot on the ceiling hoping it is a portal to the energy I need to drag myself out of bed. I get up, walk into my son's bedroom. He says, 'I had an accident.' I fight back the groan and pick up the packet of wipes next to the bed. I tell my boy that it is all right and that accidents happen. As in the version above, I sling him over my shoulder and we make our way to the shower. In the meantime the baby has woken up and one of the other kids is nagging Marilynn about when breakfast is going to be ready. The slogan 'Real Men Are Real Mad' comes to mind as the clock on the wall reads 6.15 a.m.

I used to believe that being a 'real man' was about being tough in a lumberjack kind of way. Don't get me wrong, part of me would love to be a lumberjack. I have no doubt that lumberjacks are strong and resilient. But I have been stretched and prodded in a myriad of ways that test my manhood, in ways I never imagined I could be until I had kids. And it's not only in the interaction with my kids, but in the relationship with my partner too. The mother of your children is so easy to forget and so easy to neglect – yep, plenty of guilt about this. But hey, I am jumping ahead: let us start at the beginning.

Getting Pregnant

Dear God, she's pregnant.

I'd heard the horror stories. The beautiful, subtle young woman you fell in love with would turn into a horrendous creature that wanted to do nothing but swell and vomit.

And what about me, about to become a dad! Do I really have the right, the responsibility or even the attention span to care for the life of another? Sure, the geranium my mum let me choose from the garden centre when I was nine is still doing fine, but I had a sinking feeling that this might be different.

My introduction to parenthood was a little unconventional. When I met Marilynn she already had a child, Kalym, from a previous relationship. With 'Mr Biological's' part in this little three-year-old's life well and truly over, Marilynn was wary of a reliance on men, emotionally or financially. Still, we took the plunge into marriage. Before I knew it she was pregnant with the honeymoon baby – and the honeymoon was only two days long. In retrospect, I had no idea what I was doing – but what soon-to-be Dad does?

Faced with being the major male figure in a three-year-old's life and soon to be a dad to a newborn, I had to find a solution. What to do? I did what many of us do inadvertently – I drew upon what I thought I knew. I tried to be an 'instant-dad' to Kalym and got knocked back again and again.

This was Major Mistake Number One. I was attempting to be something that I was not – yet.

Maybe this is why babies are born so small and can't see properly. If they saw that look of fear, worry and love upon your face the first time you were left alone with them, it wouldn't exactly instil a sense of confidence in their tiny body. I am just lucky that Kalym let me learn to be Dad along the path of building our relationship. Not only is my name on his birth certificate, as the adoption finally came through, but I *feel* like his dad. It even took a while to feel like Dad for Lachy, though he was biologically mine, but then newborns don't seem to notice as much.

So I'd say go with your instinct. You know what feels right, and I believe that if you are a concerned parent 99 per cent of the time this will be better than following some other person's philosophy that they shove down your throat.

The pregnant partner

Playing poker-face for a two-day-old baby is one thing, but what about the woman you love who is undergoing 'changes'? Can you remain focused when she asks, 'Do you still think I'm beautiful?' Rather than replying, 'For goodness sake, of course I do. I just have no idea how I am going to do this Dad thing!' you reply, as you should, 'Yes, of course, sweetie/dear/angel.'

It is natural that Marilynn wanted affirmation about how she looked when she was pregnant. She was understandably paranoid that I might find her ugly. The truth was I didn't really think about it – *she was still her and beautiful, just pregnant.* And I was still me, but pretty soon I was about to turn into a father. I was terrified and numb and excited.

Which brings me to Wisdom Number One. I can't remember where I heard it and I know that I have heard it from more than one person, which means I can't pass it off as my own:

Mum looks after Baby, Dad looks after Mum.

Focus on that. Trust me, it helps in the whole process. It is probably something that you are okay with, otherwise you would have been given the flick a long time ago. The safer she feels with you, the more she can be a mother and let you ease into the Dad role. This process begins the moment that test-strip reads positive.

I have watched Marilynn cope through several pregnancies and, I must admit, it does not look very comfortable. Not being able to sleep on your front, nausea, back pain – it is bad enough to watch. Weaker sex, yeah right. Then again, I have heard of women who love being pregnant, and say that they 'never felt better' – that's fantastic. Just don't bank on this being your beloved. On the three occasions I have heard this from women, I ask, 'So why didn't you have more kids?' Every reply was the same. 'My husband wouldn't let me.' Go figure.

If it is any consolation to her, I don't care about my wife's stretch marks or any other physical change associated with pregnancy and childbirth, and yes, having my children does make me love her more. But as the physical changes are immediately apparent to her, *reassure her.* It may not be important to you because you feel as though you are just waiting for the bomb to go off. Strange creatures, these pregnant ladies. Enjoy them when they feel good and shut up and do as you're told when they don't. This may not be traditionally 'manly', but what kind of idiot looks down the barrel of a gun to see if it is loaded? Or, for that matter, what 'good man' does not look after his mate when she is feeling at her worst?

Looking after your mates, especially your best one, makes you more of a real man in my books.

The Big Day

Then comes the day. Quick birth, slow birth, home birth, hospital birth or back-of-the-Kingswood birth, one way or another the thing comes out. In speaking to my father, who has five children, I learned that he got to witness only my birth. He said it was an amazing experience.

I was lucky enough to be at the birth of my three littlest and to actually deliver my now four-year-old. Absolutely nothing prepared me for this. It is never nice to see anyone you love in pain and that is exactly what childbirth is – pain. Yes, I have heard the stories of painless birth using crystals, mantras or heavy drugs. Neat. But in my admittedly limited experience I have never seen a woman have a baby without some element of pain. I was lucky just to suffer from sleep deprivation during the birth of my children; by all accounts some men are abused, ignored or end up with crushed fingers in the process of comforting their loved one as the waves of pain continue to roll in.

I don't pretend to be an expert, but some things to me seem just common sense when aiding your wife in this process:

Don't leave unless you have to. It's not about you, it's about her. Ducking off for a beer or a game of touch with your friends is really not the way of showing empathy or understanding.

Let no one into the room that she does not want to be there. Apart from possibly a medical professional in times of need. This group of 'get outs!' includes: medical students (you don't have to let them be there!), any other doctor who wants to assert his or her importance over your midwife who is doing a great job by herself, mothers-in-law, sisters, spiritual healers, tea ladies or mates.

You are the Number One advocate for your partner.

As she concentrates on holding back the burning white pain, your job is to be there, whether it takes one hour or 50. From laughing to screaming, go with it. If you are there for her during this time, it will

227

bring you closer together than ever. Forget about the torrent of abuse, nail marks and crushed fingers.

Having a morbid curiosity I decided to go 'tail-end' at the final stage of the first birth I'd witnessed – and then again at the second, at my wife's request. I couldn't have gone 'head-end' and reported how well she was doing. It was surreal, but not unnatural. There is something about being right there at the moment your baby faces the world that stirs the protective streak in you. The hang-ups you may have had about seeing 'that' happen to 'that' quickly disappear when your eyes become fixed on this new little part of you.

And from that point you are basically smitten, and blessed. Nothing has taken me to the extremes that raising children has. Nothing else has plunged me to the depths of complete inadequacy, raised me to complete adulation or left me in complete exhaustion.

So You're Now a Dad

It is at about this point that everyone around you will start telling you specifically what you are doing wrong. Don't think that you're alone with this. Chances are that your partner has had it for close to nine months – 'In my day . . .', 'You should always . . .', 'I can't believe you chose to . . .' Blah blah blah. From names to socks, you are bound to have it wrong.

One of the first things you need to realise as a new or recurring parent is that guilt is really not that necessary. You will feel it, but I take comfort from the fact that if I am feeling a little guilt it at least means that I must be thinking about how I am raising my children. I believe that some of those that are guilt-free haven't really thought about the consequences of what they are doing to their children, so feel nothing at all. *A bit of guilt is okay; it just reinforces the fact that you care.*

So there you stand – the man, the father, the head of the house. A person who has always been in control. You may have a successful career and enjoy the respect of your peers, then in wanders this little soul who couldn't care less whether you are a banker or a ballerina. Sure, we all have aspirations for our kids, but isn't the key that essentially they are going to love you for whoever you are? What a deal! And what do you have to do in return?

Well, you have to love them no matter who they are. This is my admittedly simplistic philosophy. I try to avoid placing my hang-ups on my kids, but this can be really hard. For instance, probably like a lot of fathers, I have delusions of grandeur for my 'boys' (I haven't yet formulated these for my daughter, apart from the fact that she will not be dating until her 30s). Every time I see my three-year-old kick a ball, he is pegged in general terms as a fantastic sportsman. But I try not to project my hang-ups. Sometimes I fail. But I try.

Then, as your kids get a bit older, you are supposed to spend all your spare time with them. You feel guilty when you are at work, or maybe you get defensive when you are told that you spend all your time at work – but you *have* to work! Just about every parenting book, magazine, pamphlet and anecdote I have read or heard tells us how much we would like to spend all our time with our kids and how we don't get to see them enough. This is true in theory, but have you ever tried spending all day and every day with your kids? I know I find this very difficult.

When you do, it usually seems as though there is no balance in your life. If you are someone who can do it and love it, fantastic. A friend of mine does it and is by all accounts the perfect 'house dad'. But I don't think that it is realistic that *all* people should be expected to want to do so.

So give a little empathy for your partner at home if you are at work all day. The days of coming home and putting your feet up and reading the paper while the wife keeps the kids quiet are over, especially if you want them to talk to you when they are teenagers. You may be the only source of adult conversation that your partner has had all day, so shut up about yourself when you come in the door and listen to the little triumphs and trials of *her* day – your corporate merger can wait.

And don't feel guilty for wanting time away from your kids, even if you don't spend all that much time during the week with them. Bear this in mind and I reckon there will be times when you really want to play 'cars' or 'shopping' with them. You do, however, need to adjust some of your pre-kid priorities and no child comes without sacrifice and change.

The testicular disadvantage

Then one day you feel that you are doing it right. You reckon you have a bit of a handle on this parenting thing. You're spending quality time with the kids. You're giving your wife some alone time, and you are enjoying the whole dad thing. But no matter how good you think you are doing as a father, you are at one immediate disadvantage. Let's face it: *You're a guy. What do you know compared to any woman?* You may never be able to match the knowledge of a woman who has raised children (though personally I think you can), and you will never actually *be* a woman and give birth or breastfeed – but don't undervalue what you do know, and *never use it as an excuse not to get involved.*

I remember when Kalym, our oldest, was about three-and-a-half and Lachy, the next kid, was just born. We had just purchased our first car and Marilynn had the audacity to suggest that I take them both out so she could have a sleep. What was she thinking? *I can't take both children! I don't know what I am doing! I'm not a woman! I wasn't born with some innate understanding of child-raising!* I look back to that situation and think, what a chicken.

Don't buy into the game of being an inadequate male, just because you are a man. No matter how hard you try, though, you will still face the prejudice. My wife and I were in the supermarket a while back and had the four kids with us. We came across an acquaintance. I am not exactly sure of the conversation that followed, but it seems that some women are like iron filings – give them a charge and they all stick together. From the conversation came the implication that I was finding some aspects of child rearing difficult. Out poured from this woman's mouth: 'Well, Tony, you just need to learn that kids are like that!'

This woman has no children of her own and no dealings with them on a day-to-day basis. I am not an aggressive person, but if I had had a can opener at the time, the Italian peeled tomatoes would have ended up on her head.

It becomes more complex if the woman has borne nine children and is 85 years old. In the supermarket one day, holding my fourth child (then a baby), I was accosted by one 'experienced' mother, 'She needs a hat – she'll freeze.' The reply I gave I probably deserve to be punished for. 'Please, lady, this is my fourth baby. I do have some idea what I am doing.' But this was nothing in comparison to what I was thinking of saying to shut her up: 'I am trying to give her hypothermia – I'm sick of the crying.'

What the woman in the supermarket failed to see is that no parent, man or woman, who really cares would wish any emotional, physical or any other kind of harm on their kids, because nothing brings out the protective instincts like being a parent.

Perspective and Sacrifice

It is truly amazing what frustrates you as a parent that you may never have considered before. It is not only what the kids do (which is obvious and constant), but what those who do not have kids do. It is a pointless exercise in getting mad with these people. All of us have been childless at some point, so simply change your perspective.

Many of my friends are childless at present. When we, or they, visit, I am amazed at the way they say, 'I am just going to pop out,' and they do. No car seats, buckles, shoes on/off, drink of water, taking a toy – the list goes on. Logistically, the stuff you never thought of amazes me – so you change your perspective. And if you let this happen, your priorities change too. Stuff I used to worry about having or doing has lost its importance. Sure, there is stuff that I miss and sometimes I resent the repetitive stuff I have to do, but I look at those things as the hard yards. *Do the hard yards and you will get the rewards* – love, respect and being the centre of someone else's universe (at least until they go out of orbit as a teenager, but that's another story).

Being a dad, we get to touch that raw side of life – the bits that seem to be important. We can't really articulate why, but helping these small pieces of yourself develop in this chaotic world seems to have a bit more importance than the racing stripes down the side

231

of your car or being able to drink a dozen in under an hour.

So here comes Wisdom Number Two:

Get over yourself – they will love you for who you are.

They won't love you for the racing stripes or sculling record. Ultimately they love you for the love you give them. Make them safe and valued. Involve them, when you can, in the things that you love to do, or even have to do.

Lachy and Malachy love to help me clean the car. Kalym helps me with the lawn mowing. Sure, it is very messy. The car occasionally gets whacked by a cleaning implement, the lawn remains uncut in a variety of areas and it takes five times as long, but better to do it this way than sit around resenting the kids because you can't get it done and then you don't get it done anyway.

Nothing but child-raising has made me feel so out of control, but made me feel so much like an adult. I look back and realise I was once pretty wrapped up in my own world. Now my world revolves around a whole bunch of little people. If you can, though, hold on to some of the constants you have enjoyed throughout your life. I say if, because sometimes these things may just be unfair.

A friend of mine was obsessed with golf. Every weekend he would play without fail. One Sunday morning I saw him out walking with his three-month-old. I asked him how the sacred round of 18 was yesterday. He told me that he had not played and might not for a wee while. I asked, 'Why? Golf is your life!' He quite simply said, 'I can get that back anytime.' What a real man, I thought.

If you really need this time, you should try and get it, but not at the expense of your number-one priority – the family.

Marilynn was finding that I was really stressed out on the weekend, even when I didn't have other work to do. We had three pre-schoolers and I had given up running so I could help out. She sent me out for a run one Saturday morning and took the boys for a walk. After the run, I felt set up and relaxed for the weekend. I didn't expect it but I certainly appreciated it. Herein lies the problem for men. If you are at work all week you give yourself to your job. You get home and you feel that you should give to your kids and partner. But you also feel you deserve some *me* time, and surely you do – but then you think, so does my wife. The answer is sacrifice. It just has to happen. The ability to put your kids and wife first is part of being a real man. It won't last forever, and if you are lucky enough to have support through grandparents, family and friends, use it. You are not neglecting your children if you do – they will benefit from interacting with others and it will give you some well-deserved time out.

So what is being a real man? I used to think it was about all the testosterone-soaked images I grew up with: drinking large amounts of beer, driving a fast car, hanging out with hot chicks and to some degree being a pseudo-intellectual tosser. These days, I fall asleep after about two beers, I drive a people-mover, hot chicks are what I get at KFC and I realise that knowing Act One of *Hamlet* off by heart is not a definitive mark of intelligence.

Still, I feel like more of a real man than I ever have. I have more patience than I have ever had before, I feel love in a way that I have never felt, I have tested the boundaries of my physical abilities, failed at times and bounced back. More important, I feel that not only could I endure massive physical pain for my children and would do anything to protect them, but that I can comfort, reassure and applaud them in the highs and lows of their lives.

Go on – be a real man.

Code TWELVE

THE OLD CODE: Equality

It's a nice ideal to imagine that everyone is equal. It is nice to imagine that everyone has the same opportunities and possibilities open to them. But it is an ideal based on fiction rather than fact.

Equality between men and women does not exist once children are involved. Until some day in the distant future when men can become pregnant, a woman is the only one who can carry a child. Only women can breastfeed. Therefore women are required to move out of the workforce, however briefly. They don't have the same opportunity to pay back student-loan debt as men. After time out of the workforce, they will generally re-enter on a lower salary than their male partner.

Equality between adults does not exist once children are involved. A couple with no children is very different from one with children – not least of which are the financial differences. Equality appeals to a group who would like to believe that everyone is the same, when we are not. The ideal of equality only serves to punish women and children and families.

We need to dump this code and move to a far more sensible one: equity.

THE NEW CODE: Equity

In 1990, the UN Convention on the Rights of the
Child became international law. If you read this
document, you would find a lot of assumptions.

*Convinced that the family, as the fundamental group of society and
the natural environment for the growth and well-being of all its
members and particularly children, should be afforded the necessary
protection and assistance so that it can fully assume its responsibilities
within the community:*

*'Recognising that the child, for the full and harmonious development
of his or her personality, should grow up in a family environment, in
an atmosphere of happiness, love and understanding . . .'*

The statements in this document, so succinctly and eloquently written, cover the ultimate human-rights issue. I believe they need to be read and reread, pasted on walls and displayed for all to see.

They provide the premise from which we should judge our governments – how does the government treat the *family*? Are parents forced to work too many hours? Are children denied the right to have access to their parents due to pressure for new parents to return to work when the children are at increasingly younger ages?

I've spent many an hour reading parliamentary debates, especially those that are to do with the rights and responsibilities of parents. There are some politicians who say that no support should be given to parents, that no baby is a surprise – a parent has nine months to prepare for it. This lack of surprise is used to justify opposing paid parental leave.

We may bring up issues of what the government may do with crime, race, education, economics and so on, but it all starts with the family. If families are pushed to their limits because of inadequate wages and high taxes, student-loan debt and lack of family support, then the result, quite obviously, is a breakdown of the family. Such pressures cause conflict between parents and their children, and set the stage for desperation and its consequences – divorce, violence, malnutrition, inadequate housing and health care.

When the family is not acknowledged, the government is denying the right of parents to parent. More importantly, it denies our children the right to grow up secure in their family. It is mistreating *the fundamental* group of society.

Why is the family the fundamental group?

Quite simply, the fate of our nation rests on the shoulders of the next generation.

Parents have their work cut out for them. It is no small feat to suffer sleep deprivation for years, to make sacrifice after sacrifice for our children, to take responsibility for a precious wee life or lives.

We carry the guilt of living in a nation where children are being failed. We know that children these days are more aggressive, more prone to violence, expecting instant gratification, unable to differentiate between right and wrong. We know it because almost every week we come across another child who has been murdered, has murdered, who commits some other crime or is kicked out of school. We know these children exist.

And these are just the children who make the headlines. Countless others are subjected to neglect. It is not neglect that we can put our finger on, and say, 'This child is neglected because she doesn't have adequate clothing or enough food to eat.' It is a new form of neglect, a silent form of neglect, that comes from parents who don't want to grow up, who put their own needs before those of their children, because everywhere they look they are told that they can and should have it all.

We feel the burden, and we try our best in the circumstances we've got before us. We try to provide for our children, to nurture and love them, but all the while we are battling against the price tag put on children and their parents. We battle with the idea that if we say that deep down children actually *need* their mum and dad, we are forcing women back into the isolated and deprived world of stay-at-home motherhood. In admitting this we are depriving men and women of their right to success, which is too often defined materially.

Our ability to nurture our children, to do the little things like attending the school show or watching a game of cricket or looking after a sick child, means that our needs – that is, a parent's needs – are not the same as for someone without children, or for someone whose children have grown up.

We are different.

The welfare system

There are those who believe that each family should be able to provide for itself. In an ideal world, this would certainly be wonderful.

There are some people who think that if a government gives financial assistance to families, it is creating a welfare-dependent state. Such a view, I fear, is an Americanised one, based on a kind of 'everyone out for themselves' ideology. While such an approach may help some people, we've seen it fail a large number of others.

This approach just doesn't work when it comes to having and raising children. Not all pregnancies are smooth sailing – not all women can work until the day before they give birth. Not all children are the same; some require more than others.

Children need to be nurtured. It is not a feel-good ideal but a biological reality. They need admiration, support, someone to listen, and someone to teach them. They need parents who can take a day off work to look after their child when they are sick without fear of losing their jobs.

This kind of nurturing does not provide immediate economic return – either for the parents, the children or society.

But to have a society that deprives children of their basic human rights – that is, to have a happy, healthy and nurturing family and community (and this includes extended family, childcare facilities and educational institutions) – means that they grow up in an emotionally insecure environment. The consequence of this is long-term emotional immaturity and insecurity, resulting in a fear of relationships and a lack of compassion and empathy. It results in a dog-eat-dog world from which only a small minority benefit.

Children need to move into the adult world feeling secure and knowing that developing to their fullest potential – intellectually, creatively, emotionally and physically – is something that is encouraged.

This potential originates in the family.

Government handouts

Is government-funded financial assistance for families bad for the future of New Zealand? Will it diminish our lives and make us not want to reach our full potential? Will it make us state-dependent?

Our own parents were given a Universal Family Benefit. Would all parents who received this benefit, before it was cut in 1991, consider themselves welfare-dependent? I doubt it.

Instead of being insulted by such an approach, I say that we can view state-assistance in a much more positive light: 'Hey, we realise that you are raising kids and this means that a lot of your money goes to them and that kids are expensive. We realise that unless you had children, New Zealand society would become obsolete. So, family, thanks for doing a great job. We realise that your income is not your own, that you support two, three, four or more people on that. We realise that you are making a contribution to New Zealand. So, here is our acknowledgement of that.'

While I think the Labour government in its May 2004 Budget will have changed the lives for future families, and have certainly 'put their money where their mouth is' when it comes to establishing family-friendly government policy, I would also say that they *did not go far enough*.

No, I am not a socialist, and I do think that hard work should be acknowledged, but I would like to see a return to the Universal Family Benefit – something that individual families can choose how to use.

How wonderful it would be to have a nation that adhered to the United Nations Convention, that realised that families have special needs and circumstances, that they would like to have balance in their lives and be able to work and spend time with their kids.

When the benefits (or tax credits) are tiered so tightly, one always feels on edge – will we earn too much and have to pay the money back? The same applies to childcare subsidies – although there is more scope there for earning power.

Take, for example, a family who has a financial crisis – such as a car breaking down, or needing to replace the fridge or washing machine. If one parent is at home with say, two children, they may decide to put the children into care so that they can work to bring in some more money to the home. Assume they earn $100 per day, pay their tax, potentially a student loan, then pay $30 for each child in childcare – what have they got left? Very little. So they then have to work for a month or two to cover the large bill. In the end, they've increased their income so much that they've jumped a threshold or two in the tax credits and end up having to pay the government back their (our) money. It's a bit like balancing on a very thin tightrope, and certainly contributes to family and financial stress.

A universal family allowance would eliminate this.

It would also eliminate the bureaucratic red tape and the many dollars that must be spent paying people to monitor everyone's income, chasing up those who have been overpaid or underpaid.

A flat rate would allow people autonomy, enabling those wonderful kiwi attributes such as innovation and enterprise to thrive.

A universal family benefit means that people are left with dignity. It is not: Gosh come to us and prove how poor and needy you are and we can be your guardian angel and give you money. This approach is demeaning and insulting.

How nice to have a society that acknowledges and supports the reality: happy parents make for happy kids, and happy kids make for a happy future society.

The 21st-century parent

Finally, I'd like to make some points about what we can do to advocate and nurture our children.

* Listen and learn from our children – change our perspective so that we view them from their world rather than forcing them to conform to ours.

* Make our vote count – learn about the political parties' views on the family and vote accordingly.

* Restore our confidence as experts when it comes to raising our own children.

* Spend time with our children – play with them, love them, read with them.

* Speak openly and honestly about the trials of raising children so that we can learn to support rather than judge each other.

* Realise that our children are not 'mini adults' – they cannot be dominated without long-term repercussions.

* Control the family purse strings – don't buy into the idea that our children will be happier if they have more things.

* Control technology – be aware of what our children are watching and playing so that violence does not become something that is expected and encouraged.

* Be mindful of our choices – every action has a consequence, both on an individual and at a societal level. Our nation's future depends on the choices we each make today. If we are selfish in our thinking, our children will grow to be selfish. If we base our lives on materialism, so too will our children. If we put ourselves before everyone and anyone else (including our children), so too will they venture into adulthood thinking only of what they want and how to get it.

* Encourage our children to fulfil their highest potential and in doing so to better society as a whole.

SELECTED BIBLIOGRAPHY

Byder, Linda: *A Voice for Mothers: The Plunket Society and Infant Welfare 1907–2000*, Auckland University Press, New Zealand, 2003.

Claxton, Guy: *Hare Brain Tortoise Mind: Why Intelligence Increases When You Think Less*, Fourth Estate Limited, UK, 1997.

Dahlke, Dr. Rudiger: *Everyday Initiations: How to Survive Crises Using Rituals*, Bluestar Communications, USA, 1999.

Desforges, Charles, with Abouchaar, Albeto: *The Impact of Parental Involvement, Parental Support and Family Education on Pupil Achievement and Adjustment: A literature review*, Department for Education and Skill Research Report 433, UK, 2003.

Devi, Shakuntala: *Awaken the Genius in Your Child*, Vega, Chrysalis Books, UK, 2002.

Edwards, Carolyn et al. (editors): *The Hundred Languages of Children: The Reggio Emilia Approach – Advanced Reflections*, Ablex Publishing Corporation, USA, 1998.

Freeman, Dr. Joan: *How to Raise a Bright Child*, Random House, UK, 1995.

Gardner, Dr. Howard: *Frames of Mind: The Theory of Multiple Intelligences*, Basic Books, USA, 1993.

Gardner, Dr. Howard: *Intelligence Reframed*, Basic Books, USA, 1999.

Gorman, Richard M.: *Discovering Piaget: A Guide for Teachers*, Charles E. Merrill Publishing Co., USA, 1972.

Gussin Paley, Vivian: *Wally's Stories: Conversations in the Kindergarten*, Harvard University Press, USA, 1981.

Hetherington, E. Mavis and Parke, Ross D.: *Child Psychology: A Contemporary Viewpoint*, McGraw-Hill College, International Edition, 1999.

Lee, Ruth: *The World Through Children's Eyes*, The Tauranga Moana Press, New Zealand, 1985.

Lefrancois, Guy R.: *Psychology for Teaching*, Wadsworth Publishing Company, USA, 1991.

Lewis, David: *You Can Teach Your Child Intelligence*, Souvenir Press Limited, UK, 1981.

Liedloff, Jean: *The Continuum Concept: In Search of Happiness Lost*, Addison Wesley Publishing Company, USA, 1986.

McAlpine, Don and Moltzen, Roger: *Gifted and Talented: New Zealand Perspectives*, ERDC Press, Massey University, New Zealand, 1996.

Miles, Rosalind: *The Children We Deserve*, HarperCollins, UK, 1995.

Pearce, Joseph Chilton: *Evolution's End: Claiming the Potential of Our Intelligence*, HarperCollins, USA, 1992.

Pearce, Joseph Chilton: *Magical Child*, Bantam Books, USA, 1997.

Prashnig, Barbara: *The Power of Diversity: New Ways of Learning and Teaching in New Zealand*, David Bateman Limited, New Zealand, 1998.

Rose, Colin: *Accelerated Learning*, Accelerated Learning Systems Limited, UK, 1985.

Spock, Dr. Benjamin: *Baby and Childcare*, Pocket Books, USA, 1946.

Vander Zanden, James W.: *Human Development*, McGraw-Hill, Inc., USA, 1993.

White, Piri: *Art Talk*, Oxford University Press, Australia, 1994.